DOWN THE FR(

One Man's Search for

- You know the way the watery beer throb?
- Who the hell (you think, as you sit there in some huge hangar, peering into the distance) are those ants on the stage?
- Ever bumped into a celeb and said something that made you sound like a prat?
- Ever found yourself stuck at a red light in a battered old car with ten of your mates, chased by four angry skinheads?

Over more than thirty years of gig-going, Adam Broadway has been there, done that. The Jam, Killing Joke, Deadmau5, Glastonbury, dodgy sanitation and stitches… The Prodigy, James, U2, Reading, ecstasy and embarrassment… Leftfield, The Rolling Stones, Prince, Ezio, Cambridge Junction and Brixton Academy, everyday life and Goths – and much, much more.

Along the way Adam – yes, now follically challenged and with tinnitus to boot – tells us something the shallow-callow cool-school of rock journalism never could. *He tells it like it is.*

If you ever found music really said something to you about your friends, your relationships, your dreams, *your life* – the sheer passion and honesty of *Down the Front* is here to remind you.

Join Adam for the best view in the house.
'Go on… Get down the front.'

DOWN THE FRONT

ADAM BROADWAY

© Adam Broadway 2015

First published by Imprimata 2015
This edition published by Fast-Print 2016

Adam Broadway has asserted his rights under the Copyright Designs and Patents Act 1988 to be identified as the author of this work.
All rights reserved. No part of this publication may be reproduced, stored in or introduced into a retrieval system, or transmitted in any form or by any means, (electronic, mechanical, photocopying, recording or otherwise, and whether invented now or subsequently) without the prior written permission of the publisher, or be otherwise circulated in any form, other than that in which it is published, without a similar condition being imposed on any subsequent publisher.
Any person who does any unauthorized act in relation to this publication may be liable to criminal prosecution and civil action.

A CIP Catalogue record for this book is available from the British Library

isbn 978-178456-430-8

Printed and bound in Great Britain by www.printondemand-worldwide.com

Cover design: Jane Bromham
Typeset by Mark Bracey

This book is dedicated to:-

Nick 'Nic' Crivich, for his support, passion and friendship.
Jenny for allowing me the space to travel this journey.
Ben, Phoebe and Samuel…
I hope their musical voyage is as exciting as mine.

And to every band I've ever seen… you made this book.

Set List

Soundcheck 1
One: Start! 5
Two: Fashion 19
Three: The Third Track 25
Four: Verse Four 29
Five: Support Acts 39
Six: Festivals 49
Seven: Flat Champagne and Egos 75
Eight: Down the Front 85
Nine: Born Too Young 97
Ten: Venues 109
Eleven: I'm a Celebrity… Nice to Meet You . . . 131
Twelve: Top Gigs 147
Thirteen: Rituals 167
Fourteen: The Final One 177
Fifteen: Encore 185
Sixteen: The Bonus Track 191

Soundcheck

As I walked into the market place, the crowd had pretty much dispersed. A few headed off to the kebab van for a bag of chips. The echo of someone singing the final song drifted along the narrow deserted streets. It had been a good gig tonight. The freezing winter evening made me put on the jumper I had tied round my waist earlier.

I took my normal route through Cambridge Market and headed across the small bridge over the Cam towards the Backs where I normally park on a gig night. My ears were tingling with the sound of the band, and my brain was churning over my back catalogue of past gigs. Suddenly there was a tune in my head: 'The one good thing about music is when it hits, you feel no pain… Hit me with music, hit me with music now,' – the legendary Bob Marley's "Trenchtown Rock."

'How damn true,' I thought to myself. And with that song and that thought I started to play out the story of this book. As it got colder, more and more sparks ignited in my mind. Suddenly I was in an overdrive of images, sounds and lights. It was as if, in that short but endless walk home, I was rewinding every gig I'd ever seen.

Like so many of my generation, I grew up with music. It's been at the heart of my life. I know I'm not alone. I'm sure it also touches the lives of many others. Surely there can't be anyone out there who hasn't, at some stage in their life, wiped away a quick tear, screamed themselves hoarse or argued themselves blue in the face about the meaning of some track? Whether it's "Jingle Bells," "Champagne Supernova," "Hotel California," or "Happy Birthday," music has such an amazing impact on our lives. At times it's so essential that nothing else matters. It's as important as water.

I was moved by music from an early age. And I've now been on my gigging journey for three-and-a-half decades, a long and winding road that has wiggled its way through all kinds of music from all walks of life. I've tried to be open-minded as I go, and I feel blessed to have developed broad tastes. But I have to be honest in admitting there's some stuff I simply do not *get*. While I might not turn the song off immediately, sometimes – out of respect to the artist – I do slowly ease the volume button down to zero.

Importantly, I've learnt one vital lesson. Listening to the radio and playing wonderful vinyl records (or, in my youth, listening to appallingly bad-quality tapes) was simply not enough. While I was enjoying and getting a buzz from listening to recorded music, I knew it wasn't enough. I needed to embrace the event. I needed the full experience. I needed to see it live!

I quickly learnt that seeing and hearing live music took things to another plane. I expect many of you have also been overcome by this urge to engage directly with the musicians who produced such clinically pure studio sounds. Loving listening to music was one thing but being there, seeing your idols and icons strum, holler and bash it out live, is the ultimate experience. For nearly three-quarters of my life I've been hooked; this, for me, is the ultimate trip. A trip that has led me from dingy dungeons to zeppelin-sized hangars to take in bands I love, adore or simply wanted to see. Along the way I've seen many brilliant events, but also some awful shows for which I demand a refund. However, this journey, like many in life, is a personal one. It's true too. It's *my* story. I hope you enjoy it.

I discovered the wonders of live music at an early age. I saw my first real band at 15. This is pretty average I would say. Then again, I know plenty of kids today who rock up at gigs while only just in their teens. I also have mates who boast that their kids were the youngest at festivals such as Glastonbury and so many other mega events. I also expect that quite a few of today's 'musos' were actually conceived in some cheap, cold, damp Millets tent in some wonderfully lusty field at a festival.

I bet some of you will even claim that your first ever gig was at some mighty venue seeing a world class act while you were sipping champagne in the VIP section. I wish I could say the same; in fact I'd love to claim that at my first gig I saw someone cool and trendy and they went on to rule the world. The sad thing is that I have to admit that, although I was born in 1964 and brought up on the sounds of the Beatles and early rock, my first live gig was in fact Manhattan Transfer at the Reading Hexagon. I don't mean any disrespect to Tim Hauser and the crew but – let's be honest – it wasn't the coolest of bands to see as a gig virgin.

Whether it's the many years of going to gigs or my increasingly unreliable memory, I recall only a few things from this 'my big moment.' This was when I started my journey, the night I entered a venue, handed in my ticket for inspection, and sat down in the inner sanctum – this place where people meet, laugh, drink and then dance and clap. My first ever gig.

I do recall it was a seated affair and there was a bar where you could buy a beer. Embarrassing, I know… but I think the drink had a good effect. I felt relaxed.

I didn't know what to expect. What I got was a packet of emotions sparked off by the loud, live sound, the flashing coloured lights and the roar of approval from the crowd. Not only could I *hear* all the different instruments, the way the vocals blended into each other, but I could also *see* a moving picture. There was just so much to take in. I remember the band leaving and being called back for an encore… but the rest is lost in the fog of strobe lights and a rather large mixing desk. I must have a look in the loft and hunt out their LP, in its luxury gatefold sleeve.

Seeing a band live can be – and in most cases *is* – so much fun. Over the years I've shared some fantastic times. But amongst the nights of euphoria there have also been some appalling experiences, big names that were simply rubbish, venues that reminded me of that betting shop loo scene in *Trainspotting*.

Gigging isn't always easy – as I unravel my journey you'll hear about the highs and lows. As Depeche Mode's Dave Gahan and Martin Gore put it, 'try walking in my shoes' – and remember this is a trip. Enjoy yours.

One: **Start!**

There was fifteen million fingers
Learnin' how to play
And you could hear the fingers pickin'
And this is what they had to say…

"Let There Be Rock" by AC/DC

FOR ME, SEEING A BAND PLAY LIVE isn't just about the music. It's a complex mixture of experiences. It's about the venue, the support act, the light show and the moments before that roadie at the back of the stage wiggles his torch to say 'Dim them lights, the band are coming on.'

There are certain venues that take a band's meticulously produced tunes – those clean sounds you hear through your CD or MP3 player in today's modern, crisp and precise world – and simply explode them into another dimension. (Of course in my early years the sound we grew up with was neither clean nor pure. On the vinyl records I would quickly learn to love and cherish, it was often mixed rather simply and muffled with dust and scratches.) Couple this with the gradual build-up of anticipation from a crowd of similar-minded folk from all walks of life, add in the pre-event backing tracks and *that* moment when the house lights are snuffed out and the crowd roars as the band enters the stage.

It must be daunting. The first note sets the scene. The band have to enter their stage with an air of authority and a genuine interest in wanting to meet their fans' expectations. It's not a time to slip up, which I'm pleased to report I've never seen, though I did see Gryff Rhys Jones fall off the stage in Oxford.

As time passes and gigs fade away, every element of the event becomes more and more important. Like most things, the more experience you have of gig-going, the more you start to analyse it like some chemistry experiment. Or do you? Surely the whole point is to let the experience evolve and then you can become a critic at the end – after the encore has faded away, and the house lights are turned on; after you trample across the zillions of crushed plastic cups, dodge the pools of lager and the security politely usher you home.

That said, I can't actually recall the very first note at my first ever live gig. I was like any novice in a new place. I followed what I thought were the rules. I arrived on time. In fact I was so eager not to miss anything that I arrived in plenty of time, ready and expectant. The first *real* band (Manhattan Transfer are excluded for reasons of street credibility) I saw live in a real venue was a band from Dulwich called Random Hold. They were never massive in the UK but to me they were. It was to them that I claim I lost my gig virginity. While the MT gig was like petting behind the bike sheds, Random Hold were the real thing. Full on, intimate, passionate, and with the lights off.

The gig was on Sunday, 25 November 1979.

Random Hold were a four-piece post-punk indie band – typical of this time. They had an album *View from Here* with tracks entitled "The Blind," "Central Reservation" and "Silver Spoons." If they ever had a hit track it was "Montgomery Clift," from their US *Etceteraville* album. Their show was simple but effective. They produced a clear clean sound and I loved it. They could have played anything that evening as I had never heard of them before, but as they progressed through their short set I drew closer to them and started to take in and enjoy their sound. Soon I was bopping around, singing completely random lyrics, but absolutely full of it. I was immersed. I was hooked. Of course I was; it was my first real live band and I was there.

Looking around I was not alone. Ok, not everyone was dancing like Mr M. Jackson, but there were plenty of nodding heads and a slight movement of feet and some bodies bouncing gingerly skywards. A few of us were entranced. Of course my jumping for joy was also driven by that magical sensation, though I couldn't admit it at the time: I was here at a gig watching a real band playing live. I wanted to celebrate the event. I was free. I was at a live event and buzzing.

The venue for this gig was the Reading Hexagon. The Hexagon still exists; at the time it was a modern building near the town centre in one of those classic 1970s shopping and office complexes that were designed to change our shopping habits. Johnny Rotten could have been thinking about it when he sang 'your future dream is a shopping scheme.' It would never have won a design award but at least it provided a new entertainment venue amongst the concrete and boredom of a town like Reading. Like most shopping centres, it was a cold, windy and hostile place, especially for a young wannabe muso out after dark.

I arrived by bus: the number 21. Conveniently, it stopped outside the new Thames Valley Police HQ so I felt reasonably safe. By now I was a veteran solo traveller on public transport – for eight years I had been travelling to and from school on local buses.

But attending a gig without my parents was so different. I did have a schoolmate with me but we were both new to this gigging game. We were in the concrete jungle late, in the dark and virtually alone. There was no CCTV and evening café culture was only something you did on your two-week summer holiday. This was also a time when football hooliganism was ugly and pandemic. The youth were rebelling and anyone was a target.

Rob and I walked quickly to the venue. A sign above the entrance gave us confidence. The band's name was up there in lights. We headed for the entrance, which I recall was more like a theatre. Then again, the Hexagon was a multi-venue place. One night it would be punk, then opera, then a touring orchestra, then rock. It was 1979.

The doorman greeted us warmly, checked our tickets and tore a bit off. We were in. My first real gig. Once in, we headed straight to the bar and bought a beer. It was easy to do back then. The beer was nothing special; gig venues rarely supply decent beers. There was no Brakspear's on tap in those days.

After a few sips we headed into the main auditorium; standing was downstairs. We actually had seat tickets in the balcony but could simply walk unchallenged into the open area in front of the stage. The seats were set out in a half-hexagon around and above the reasonably large empty space. It felt different downstairs. This one minor gate-crash started off my passion for standing at gigs – as you will hear later. There was hardly anyone there because it was in fact 7:34 pm and the doors had only just opened. Only first-timers arrive at gigs on time. Rock or indie gigs aren't like a play or orchestral concert when everyone has to be seated on time or they risk not being let in. Gigs are different. The bands say when they're coming on and how long they would play for. Or at least they used to. These days they're heavily contracted to be precise about what and when they play. But I wasn't to know this. The pure excitement of wanting to see a live gig meant that nothing could be taken for granted. I didn't want to miss a thing.

So there I was, standing in a near-empty auditorium with a beer in my hand with my mate, Rob, waiting for the support act to appear. We knew nothing about them, but what they didn't know either was that by simply being here in a concrete cathedral in the middle of Reading they were going to come on to the stage, play live music and change my life. Random Hold duly appeared and with minimal fuss played what I recall as being a pretty solid set. As soon as they finished I rushed over to the merchandise stall to find out who they were.

With the confidence I've always found to be a good thing when trying to not look *quite* such a prat, I naively asked the merchandise bloke: 'Who were the support act?'

'Random Hold.'

'Oh yeah. Thanks,' I gratefully replied and walked away. I didn't give the game away that I had never heard of them. 'I'll have to check them out in next week's *NME*,' I said to myself.

The main act was, by this time in late 1979, almost a household name. They not only had a Top Ten hit in the bag but they were also local. Well almost. They came from Swindon, which in footballing terms was a local rival; if and when the Biscuit Men (aka the Royals, aka Reading FC) played them, there was certainly plenty of trouble and police crowd control was much needed. But music works on a different level to sport; it is and remains a way to bond. For us Reading folk we held nothing against XTC, in fact we loved it that a band from 'around our way' was a success and playing at our Hexagon.

"Making Plans for Nigel" is such a catchy tune. I only heard it once on the radio in a car going to school and the very next day

I was down the local record shop buying it on seven-inch vinyl. So imagine my delight when the local radio station, Radio 210, announced that XTC were planning to play in our lovely concrete Hexagon. Immediately I thought, 'I'm up for that.' But how? Back in those early days, getting tickets was altogether a completely different adventure. We didn't have Ticketmaster, See Tickets, eBay or Get Me In. You got tickets by going to the box office in person or sending in a letter with a stamped addressed envelope. We didn't have computers and the venues didn't have deals with agents offering telephone sales. It was easy then! I just had to go to the box office in person and get the tickets myself. But I was a schoolboy, all satchels and appalling handwriting. To make matters worse, my school was out of town. In fact miles from bloody anywhere, so there was no chance of bunking off at lunchtime.

So I did what any other kid would do. I asked my mum to get the tickets.

'Mum, are you going into town today?' I said, with a mouth full of cereal.

'Yes. Why?'

'Any chance you could get me and Rob a couple of tickets for a concert at the Hexagon?' I asked, teeth gritted and fingers crossed.

'Yes.' The reply was music in itself.

Amazingly, she happily obliged. Thinking back, I never did pay her back the £2 ticket price. Thanks, mum, because if you hadn't traipsed across town, I would never have gone. Then again, get real. I would have found a way to get the tickets. Wouldn't I?

XTC were a class act. For me they were one of the original so-called 'New Wave' bands. They had style, used more electronic keyboards than guitars and Andy Partridge had a quirky voice. They played a full set with an encore. The sound and light show was a stunning new experience for me and lifted all the hits on their well-crafted album to another level. It was a bit raw in parts and certainly much louder than I could ever play the album at home. And rather than tapping the beat out on my bedroom floor I had the chance to jump around with random fellow-maniacs. Sadly XTC were never going to be in my Top Ten of live gigs, but they were the reason for my first real live gig, and for that I'll be ever thankful. To this day, whenever they come on the radio or TV I smile to myself and say silently 'I was there.'

On the way home I tried to play it all back. I tried vainly to re-create the whole experience. I wanted to remember it all and decided from that moment that I would make a list of all the bands I would see and collect all my gig tickets, which is true to this day.

But like a lion who has tasted flesh for the first time I wanted more. I knew then that I wanted – in fact *needed* – to see more bands live. Something had sparked inside me. I was on the start of a very long and twisted journey. But who should I see next?

You may be surprised but I got off to a slow start with my new venture. 1980 was my probationary year. My first task was simply to clock up a few more valuable gigging points. But, being a timid schoolboy, it was six months before I would enter another auditorium, see the house lights go out and then close my eyes and let my ears resonate to some well-constructed sound, blasting out from a large rack of speakers. I didn't play it simple, though. My next gig was to see the guitar hero Carlos Santana playing "Black Magic Woman" and "She's Not There" (among many of his blossoming catalogue of hits) at Wembley Arena. This genius guitarist had that remarkable quality of making an instrument made of wood and metal scream like a wild beast. To this day, though, I'm not sure what enticed me to travel half way across London to see him. Afterwards I remember feeling slightly let down, even though his band at the time was made up of some of the world's best musicians. I just couldn't quite put my finger on it. This gig business wasn't going to be easy.

Being 16 wasn't either. There was so much rushing through my tiny head: emotions, hormones, desires, shyness, growing up. What was certain was that I found comfort and hope in music. Gigging was becoming my escape. For 1980, collecting and expanding my musical taste without the need to be tribal was my salvation. I clocked in my apprentice card at four further gigs in this my first full year, proudly brought to its end with the show everyone was talking about: Pink Floyd's *The Wall*. (More about that later.) Crucially, this new venture was helping me to find a freedom to roam, only held back by youthful innocence, a dependence on public transport and limited pocket money. I looked back over the year and decided to award myself a merit for my probationary period. I had survived and so I was off to big, live music school.

Toyah Wilcox turned up on my radar at exactly the right time.

Toyah was the petite female punk with a slender figure and rather sexy lisp. At this time I expect there were many boys' bedroom walls adorned with posters of Toyah and/or Debbie Harry. So my heart started to race when I found out she was touring. Toyah, by 1981, was becoming a major star, especially for those interested in the post-punk movement. Her music was catchy and punchy, which drew a mixed bag of followers including punks, New Wave indies and skinheads. But besides her sex appeal she was also experimental and arty. Toyah's stage shows on *Top of the Pops* were unforgettable, a kind of female Ziggy Stardust.

She was due to play the Rainbow Theatre, near Finsbury Park. This was North London, John Lydon territory. While North London was not exactly my manor, but it was accessible by tube via the 'Picc-a-dick-ally' Line, as it was affectionately called.

The gig was on 21 February 1981. I was excited by this new trip and new venue. Trips to London from the west were like an away match. I always felt a slight nervousness about travelling to London but this time I was overflowing with adrenaline, something I hadn't quite felt yet about seeing a gig. Away trips added to the event experience, a sense of adventure. Rob and I hardly spoke. We were getting more excited with every tube station we went through.

We arrived at Finsbury Park and headed out under the massive East Coast Mainline railway bridge, which was poorly lit and dripping with smelly water. Finsbury Park oozed poverty. We decided to avoid the Sir George Robey pub which offered the chance of a sneaky beer. I found out years later that the Sir George Robey was a music venue in its own right, famed for hosting punk and metal bands. John Lydon frequented the place which I learnt that my football mate, Dave's dad owned at one point. As two naive would-be musos, we kept our heads down and made straight for the venue – luckily only a few yards away. A majestic, white-tiled 1930s ex-cinema, the main doors are up a few steps at the front; tickets checked and we're in.

The main hall turned to the right and offered a large open space sloping down to the stage, which was surrounded by huge black drapes. The support act was Huang Chung, who were ok but didn't inspire me.

Around nine, to huge cheers from the crowd, Toyah and her band emerged. We pushed forward and by the second note we were all pogoing up and down. Looking around, everyone was jumping on the spot in time, soaking up Toyah's mayhem. It was a gig of hits because, like many new bands, their set list comprised only enough tracks to fill two sides of black vinyl.

My Toyah gig was gig number six. I was trying to learn fast the tricks of this new craze. As the gig was in February I had arrived nicely wrapped up in my Arthur Daley coat… stylish, hey! Anxious about getting the last train and not wanting it nicked, I decided to keep my lovely warm coat on. Sensible, I reckoned. What I hadn't thought through was that pogoing around a crowded venue with my muso pals meant I would get hot. Very hot.

By the fourth track I was sweating profusely. But I was in a good position and enjoying the gig. I wasn't going to move, and certainly not back to the cloakroom.

Then I did the classic. I turned to the guy next to me and, feeling full of gig confidence, 'great gig. It ain't 'alf 'ot though,' I said naively in some fabricated London accent.

'Well take your coat off then!' he replied rather sensibly. He didn't say it but I knew exactly what he thought. 'Prat!'

Toyah signed off with a screaming 'Ieya' and the crowd went mental. Gig over, Rob and I pegged it out of the venue and charged off to the tube. I was still in my sheepskin coat and now drenched. We crossed the busy Seven Sisters Road and headed along the foot tunnel down to the tube. The tiled walls were dark yellow, dripping with years of tobacco smoke. You could smoke on the tube and virtually everywhere at this time.

I remember hearing a cry down the tunnel after us. 'Oi!' We didn't look back. We just ran for our train, and once on board we looked at each other, smiled and said 'Great gig.'

I felt that the Toyah gig had completed my probationary period. Now I could start to claim professional membership of this unique club. I was now a real gig-going muso.

My parents never had a car, which slightly complicated my freedom plans as a youth. But somehow I passed my driving test first time after 12 lessons. I always look back to this little miracle. It was probably the first real goal I ever set out to achieve. Learning to drive would be my lottery prize. My schooling had rubbed off on my innate competitiveness – the desire not to be outdone wasn't so bad after all.

The year started well but the next gig I remember took me into the open air. While the Random Hold and XTC gig was my first, it was indoors, and it was time to sample the great outdoors. I was, by now, listening to music whenever and wherever I could. I was also blessed because so much diverse music was appearing left, right and centre. One of the earliest outdoor events I went to see was the Summer in the City festival held at the Crystal Palace Bowl. The Bowl was a lovely venue where the stage was set in a naturally formed basin with a large pond in front. The Summer in the City event was my first real taste of a number of elements relating to this whole gig experience thing.

My school was set in the Berkshire Downs, Kate Middleton country, to the west of Reading. But the Summer in the City gig of 1982 was in Crystal Palace, London, which was famed for its running track and a Division Two (at that time) football team. It was also south (or should I say 'sarrff'?) of the river, which was new territory. A place I had never been to and only heard of with some fear.

Now, my dad is a Cockney and all my London adventures were 'norff' of the river. South London was this new planet where different tribes, clans and gangs hung out. It was a fearsome place where, to some, everything was related to the Brixton Riots, everyone got mugged and there were no tube trains. All of this, of course, was and is rubbish, but this was the false image a young muso from the cosy suburbs in Reading pictured in his tiny, unbalanced brain.

So it was that a few school pals, drawn by the allure of seeing a number of top bands in a single event, decided we should venture 'sarrff'. The 1982 Summer in the City line-up was pretty cool. It featured Ultravox, Madness and Tenpole Tudor. Ok, Tenpole Tudor weren't a real pull but the other two certainly were. Both had mega Top Ten hits. Teardrop Explodes were also on the bill but for some reason didn't turn up. Maybe they had heard that Crystal Palace was this no-go area where they would be beaten to a pulp by local maundering-murdering gangs who would steal their gear and drink their hospitality rider down in one.

The second thing about this gig was the line-up itself. Eclectic band line-ups are very much par for the course today, but in the early 1980s people were still quite tribal. We still had rockers and mods. But we had new musical genres. We had punks; we had the two-tone skinhead crews, and later on we had the emerging New Romantics. Whether it was down to the economy, the rise of the Tories under Thatcher, or simply coming from rough Council estates, musos were intensely loyal when it came to musical taste. Not everyone, of course, but the hardcore fans were very focussed and extremely loyal.

Somehow a group of us decided to go and managed to get tickets. This was my mate Tim's first gig; he remembers it well today. It set him on his own gig-going journey. I was very lucky though. Not only had I managed to pass my driving test first time, I was the only pupil allowed to drive to school. And I was making a name for myself as the live music connoisseur. Luckily, I had developed a good set of loyal friends before this monumental achievement. I offered – well, we had no choice – to drive, and had arranged to pick my pals up from school rather covertly. I remember driving out of the village and pulling up near a farm gate. Suddenly four young lads jumped out from the hedge, dived into the car and off we pegged it.

It was a glorious summer's day and soon we were on the M4 heading to London, full of sprightly banter and laughter. We listened to one of the compilation tapes that I had knocked up especially for the journey. For some reason we parked miles away in Hammersmith and decided to venture in by tube, train and bus to the lovely Crystal Palace Stadium and its neighbouring bowl. We entered the bowl and, like everyone else on this glorious sunny day, sat on the grass and did what mates do best: chat away merrily, sipping the piss poor beer on offer. But we didn't care.

For some reason Madness were given the slot after Tenpole Tudor. Within a couple minutes we were all up on our feet doing the Nutty Dance to "One Step Beyond." Thumbs in mouths, playing imaginary saxophones.

'Hey you, don't watch that, watch this. This is the nutty, nutty sound of Madness. One Step Beyond,' cried Suggs. It sure was.

Perfect timing historically and it really was 'of that moment.' We loved it and so did the Nutty Boy hardcore. It was then that we noticed a load of skinheads, in drainpipe jeans, 16-hole red Doc Martens boots with yellow laces, red braces and various coloured shirts or T-shirts. They were loving it too, jumping around as if they were in the Marquee or 100 Club. But this was outside and on a scorching hot summer's day. Everyone else was soaking up the heat, lying on the grass bank. After a couple of tracks some of the skinheads were getting fed up with the side-on view of the stage – the Crystal Palace Bowl has a small lake right in front of the band. So, hot and heady after a few beers, in they went… not one but the entire gang. Soon there was a whole troupe of skinheads splashing around to the Nutty sound.

My mates and I were laughing our heads off at these nutters. We had never seen anything like it before. 'Full credit to them,' I thought. 'At least they can dry off.'

Madness were excellent. Really good value and they got everyone in the mood.

Next up were Ultravox. And there you have a clue as to what was going to happen… New Romantics were the new fad and with them came a new style. Bands such as Human League, Duran Duran and Spandau Ballet had emerged from the post-punk era and grabbed the music scene by the velvet collar. Their music was an almost instant hit with a group of teenagers too young to be rockers and too frightened to be punks. Music in the 1980s needed a new fashion, a new direction, and this was it. Ultravox had in fact been around a few years but by now were being spearheaded by the distinctive vocal (that I first heard in Slik's "Forever and Ever") of Midge Ure.

But music was still tribal. While many new musos loved the New Romantics' offer of pure sing-along pop, for the skinheads and two-tone followers, dressing up in frilly shirts and dancing without pogoing was simply not hip.

So Madness were off, the stage set was changed and on came Ultravox. We all rose and were soon dancing away.

The skinhead posse, though, had not done an Elvis and had not left the bowl. They were drying off and now needed to be entertained. Suddenly, like receiving a free pair of Doc Martens, they sensed and smelt the bait. There in front of them were a load of new musos dressed up like musketeers – it was game on.

It didn't take long. The skins went on the warpath. Charging, screaming, kicking and hitting anything with hair or a frilly shirt. People were running all over the place, or simply cowering out of view. I had seen fighting on the football terraces in the 1970s and was used to it, but never at a gig… I stood rigid, watching the fighting below.

In their boredom the skinheads simply ran amok. The ice cream man had been doing a roaring trade in the wonderful sunshine. After punching a few New Romantics, the skinheads turned their attention to his van. From the hillside I could see its 'Mind the Child' sign being rocked back and forth by this gang of some twenty skinheads. How it didn't topple over I'll never know.

Eventually a few police arrived and charged after the gang, and then everything seemed to calm down and fade away. Ultravox, with Midge at the helm, simply carried on regardless. Then they played "Vienna" and we all hugged a final waltz. The gig ended at 8.00 pm, which was surreal in itself.

We bumped away back to Hammersmith, keeping our heads down, like in the film *The Warriors* some of us had watched a few years before on an authorised school trip. We reached my car and we drove home, reflecting on the day's extraordinary events and laughing like mates do – partly out of relief that we had survived our journey '*sarrff*'.

1981 set the tone and the structure for my annual gig-going. It was wonderfully eclectic, ranging from Bob Dylan, through Duran Duran to Gang of Four. It included some venues which, as you will hear, have become temples for live music and others towards which I've developed a rabid animosity.

If there was one gig that summed it all up, at this point, it was a Monday evening in mid-December at the quainter Hammersmith venue: the Hammersmith Palais. Originally the Palais was a ballroom, and before that a factory where they built tanks. Ironically my wife Jenny's parents used to dance there, but unaware in 1981 of the serendipitous connections this place would later hold for me, I strolled up to see the gig of the year.

The Palais was a large room with the main stage on the far side. There was nothing really special in appearance about it except that everyone stood up and could get a great view of the stage. It was hot inside, a complete contrast to the bitter cold on the street.

Tonight it was The Jam. If there was one band that united the youth, who became involuntary historians, it had to be The Jam. There was arguably more energy, angst, calm, passion and honesty in this one band than in anything else around at this time. I arrived early and was expecting to see Bananarama. Not a band I would have immediately associated as a support act. Lots of high-pitched fancily dressed girls singing to a mainly hardcore mod following of young blokes seemed a bit risky. But they were a no-show. So we waited to see the next support act, who were TV21. I took to them straight away. They had a great guitar sound and reminded me a bit of Random Hold.

It was nearly Christmas, and cold outside. There was the expectation that this was going to be a night to remember. The crowd were boisterous, well-oiled and already very sweaty. The Jam, all three of them, jumped onto the stage and went straight into a blistering opener, "The Gift," followed by "Down in the Tube Station at Midnight." If a venue could ever explode, the Palais was close to it. I looked around; the whole floor was pogoing in unison. Hundreds of heads of all shapes and sizes bouncing up and down. We were given a full set of hits and everyone seemed to know the lyrics even to the lesser-known B sides. "I Wish I Could Be Like David Watts" summed it all up.

The set seemed to fly past. Of course it would, with tracks typically averaging three-and-a-half minutes. I didn't want it to end. But it did. I was so lost in the event I can't even recall if there was an encore. I just found myself standing in the Palais, ears ringing, T-shirt soaked, knackered. My eyes were glazed over as if in a trance. I came round smiling and then suddenly I welled up. Strangely I wanted to cry. I wanted to let it out. I had gone through a musical trip and knew this was it. I wanted more. I had seen an almost perfect gig and the bar had been raised. This was it. Gigging was the ultimate buzz. Give me more.

Outside I stood in the entrance surrounded by mods, punks and the odd skinhead. Their faces said it all. 'Shit. That was good, very good.'

Two: **Fashion**

Quit your job 'cause I've got it made
Any time baby, let's go
Every day should be a holiday

"Every Day Should Be a Holiday" by Dandy Warhols

FASHION. I can't say it has really bothered me. Clothes are for comfort, warmth, impressing in an interview. They've never been the reason why I enjoy music. In the same way, I've never followed one specific musical style. I am, in fact, pleased that I've developed a very eclectic taste. Surely this is what music is about – you listen to music for the stimulus it gives or the mood it creates, but it doesn't matter what style or label it is. It's the music that's important. That's what matters.

Over the years, though, different musical styles have resulted in a wonderful array of dress styles and codes. Fashions and trends, while not my driver, are intricately linked to musical genres. I was too self-conscious as a youngster to get dressed up for a gig. I was too shy and reserved. But what I saw all around me was how far other musos would go. Their confidence in dressing up really set the scene and feel. I let others do the fashion thing.

The first gig where I noticed that dressing up was a part of the gig package was Hazel O'Connor at Guildford Arts Centre. My school room-mate Hugo lived near Guildford, and by 1981 – 17 and with a car – I could go wherever my wheels took me. I set off gigging with a vengeance. Hugo and I shared an interest in music and would – without thinking about it – challenge each other to find a new band or sound. With Hugo came his sister Caz and a new set of friends and potential gig-goers. So when we found out that the Top Ten starlet Hazel O'Connor (with hat) was playing in Guildford during a school holiday, it was a no-brainer. I had to go.

As typical teenagers we were incapable of making any sensible plans. Someone had my ticket; I agreed to meet whoever it was outside the venue. It was as simple and unplanned as that. The evening got off to a flyer as I found myself standing behind the Thompson Twins, wearing full New Romantic gear, in the queue at the cashpoint. They were busy laughing and enjoying themselves… I didn't interrupt.

I met up with Hugo. This would be his first ever gig – it probably had a profound effect on his musical journey that would see him seeing a gig a day for a year… more later. It was pretty easy to meet up outside the small venue. We didn't have mobiles to call or to text in order to find each other. We joined the masses in the foyer. In amongst the crowd I suddenly noticed that most people had made a real effort to dress up. I looked more intently, taking in the detail. Maybe it was the arty Guildford thing, but, reminiscing, it was more than that. The crowd was varied. Yes, there were plenty of art students dressed as New Romantics: long wavy curls, buccaneer shirts, baggy black trousers and boots. But then there were the punks dressed in Sex Pistols T-shirts, with brilliant red, green or purple hair and riddled with piercings. Then there were the skinheads in white T-shirts, red braces, light blue jeans and not a hair to cover their snarling faces. And a few fantastically colourful full-on Mohicans. Mohicans have always fascinated me. Partly out of pure jealously. I never had much hair, as if my dad's dominant gene said, 'hard luck son, you're going to be follically challenged from an early age, just like me, so don't go wasting your money on hair dye.'

I've never known anyone with a real Mohican so I've never seen or learnt what they must go through in getting ready for a gig. I can only imagine it starts with a visit to a local chemist to buy a shedload of gel and hairspray. Then hours spent in front of a mirror working on the perfect style. It must cost them a fortune. Then of course what happens the next day? How do they look the day after a hot pogoing evening down the club? Someone must know.

Picture the scene before a gig. 'Now, what colour shall I have today?' Maybe I've missed a tribal thing here… red/blue/green, each representing a different clan. Do they? I had no idea in 1981 either but I enjoyed playing it all out in my innocent head.

Hazel O'Connor, ably supported by the excellent Icehouse, drew a diverse range of styles and followers. With pints in hand we headed down the front. Within seconds of the start of the opening track we were jumping around in a mental mayhem. The skins, though, stuck together, and it wasn't long before a punch-up started. This calmed down initially but it set the theme for the night and it wasn't far into the set before Hazel had had enough. She had a bird's eye view. Enough was enough; she actually stopped the gig and told the skinheads to stop fighting. Like a strict mother or ward sister, Hazel's words hit home and surprisingly they stopped. A small cheer and applause broke out.

Musically, Hazel delivered a great sound. The band was tight and her vocals were clear and audible. She also came across as an artist on top of her game and someone who genuinely wanted the young crowd to enjoy themselves. And we certainly did. She drew us in and we sang back.

After the gig we all headed off to collect my car. Being typical teenagers, the only problem was that no one had sorted out the transport home. There were now some ten or so people wanting a lift back to Hugo's village. The bus had left a week ago. I was the only person with a car. It was a small green Volvo. A family car designed for five passengers. I called it ERD. Not wishing to let anyone down or leave them in downtown Guildford late at night, I let everyone pile in. Four in the front, five in the back and two in the boot. Unbelievable.

We slowly headed off out of town. Besides a few stragglers wandering home the place was empty. I carefully heaved my massively overladen car along towards the main road but slowed down for a red light.

One of our many passengers was Hugo's sister Caz. I'll be honest: I was a shy teenage boy. I was just starting to feel the emotions of liking another human being. I had met Caz on a couple of occasions at school and started to fancy her. I was looking forward to spending a few days with her at their pad in rural Surrey. As we neared the traffic lights, Caz decided to show off. She was innocent like the rest of us, but tried to show a hard side too. The only other people about were four skinheads on the opposite side of the street. Caz wound down the window and screamed at the top of her voice: 'I hate skinheads'…

The four young men, having had their fair share of action at the gig, heard the scream – to them it was nothing but a war cry. They took one look at each other and then at us. As quick as a light bulb they noticed we were slowing up. They started to run towards us – and fast. My heartbeat rose dramatically. Faster and faster, nearer and nearer... I've never been brave. To make things worse, I was in an overcrowded car. We were now being hotly pursued by four skinheads who were definitely in the mood to finish off their night and punch in a load of students. The red light stayed firmly red. I think I must have prayed...

As the skins, now flat out, got within twenty feet of the car, the lights suddenly turned from red to orange. I hit the accelerator – hard. ERD was no sports car, in fact it had never been driven at speed in its whole life. It was a Volvo, for God's sake. A family car not a racing machine. Now, at this point of imminent danger I was asking it to perform some Evel Knievel-type stunt. ERD leapt forward – ERD had never leapt forward before, especially with so much youthful weight inside. Weirdly I think ERD sensed the urgency and pulled away. We escaped just as one skinhead, out of pure hatred, punched the back window. Luckily it didn't break. We could hear the skins roar as we sped away...

Caz, not one to be beaten, then leaned back out of the window and shouted 'Cowards!'

We spent the rest of the journey in silence. Everyone must have been thinking the same thing. How on earth did we get out of that? Amazingly we had survived – just. I never knew why Caz had put us in so much danger. Was it bravado, being drunk or downright stupidity? It certainly wasn't the way to impress me. While music styles and fashions have since moved on considerably, I haven't seen a gig in Guildford since, out of fear I might get spotted. There are definitely times when being a coward is a good call.

Goths have always amazed me. I find it incredible what range and individuality can be achieved from just one basic colour: black. Now, black is – well, let's see – dark, plain and black. But full credit to the Goths as they manage to come to gigs in various shapes, styles, fittings and arrays, but always in black. I admit I haven't been to too many really hardcore Goth gigs. I missed the real Sisters of Mercy and bands like Bauhaus. Alien Sex Fiend never really appealed. While I liked the melody and variety many of the real

Goth bands produced, the heavier sound just didn't do it for me. Each to their own.

During my early gig-going days there were some Goth-type bands I delighted at seeing, such as The Cure, The Cult and the remaining punk bands like the mesmerising Siouxsie and the Banshees. They all pulled a large Goth following. So it was at my first The Cure gig that I saw the emerging range of Goth styles.

The female Goths caught my eye. Maybe it was their burlesque-covered frames or the fishnet stockings or their pure black hair. Boots were an essential item. Big boots, pristinely polished steel toe caps and mile-long laces.

Now, I love The Cure and to this day they remain one of my favourite bands. I first saw The Cure at my home venue at the Reading Hexagon in April 1982. This gig was the first event to make me conform to the dressing up code. Of course, with little hair, virtually no dress or style sense and not much confidence the only thing I could do was wear a black T-shirt and black jeans. It was and still remains my only way of 'signing up.' I was comfortable.

All around me the musos of various ages, sexes and sizes were dressed in black T-shirts or shirts and dark denim. It was if we were in team kit. There were no away fans; this was an event only for the home crowd. Anyone dressed in a colour looked – and was often made to feel – out of place.

The gig itself was fantastic for being so powerful, different, entrancing and near perfect. It was a great time to see The Cure. The 1980s were still early times for this great band. They had just released the *Seventeen Seconds* album and were starting to move away from those beautifully simplistic early tracks, "Three Imaginary Boys," "Killing An Arab," "10:15 on a Saturday Night." Tonight was the chance to hear the brilliant "Primary," "M," and the classic "A Forest." The Cure had become darker, more sinister and deeper. As a mixed-up teenager, these new sounds and songs hit a note even though I didn't have a clue as to what note they were hitting. The new and old tracks were duly performed with minimal lights, but they had the sheer quality of the wailing guitars and Robert Smith vocals.

In 1982 Robert Smith's voice was higher in pitch than it is today. He and the original band were dressed in black. Tonight he had short straight hair. His trademark scraggly hair and smudged lipstick were things to come. Tonight The Cure were as pure as they would ever be, even though, as a band, they were starting on a difficult journey fuelled, apparently, by loads of booze and drugs.

I remember jumping wildly around to "Primary" and "A Forest." The venue was now full of dry ice and entranced fans. I was so impressed by the gig and now so madly bonded with this amazing group of musicians that I immediately planned to see their London gig at the Hammersmith Odeon a few weeks later. This was probably as close to going on tour with a band as I'd ever get, but it was special and it meant something to me.

The Hammy Odeon (as some of us affectionately call it) gig was crammed full of every style, genre, weirdo and muso. On display was a gallery of T-shirts and merchandise promoting The Cure. I remember being tempted by a black T-shirt with the *Faith* album cover on the front. I didn't get it, but if I had, it would have been my first-ever gig T-shirt. The Hammy Odeon gig was just as stunning as the one a few weeks earlier. The Cure suited the larger stage, even though their stage set was minimalist. There were no large screens, no multiple video montages, and no strobe lights. All they had were black drapes and some coloured lights. It didn't really matter because I was deeply lost in the sound. To this day, "A Forest" is simply one of the best tracks ever made and ever played live.

Durh ning, durh ning durh ning. All I need to hear is that simple bass line.

I was now well and truly into this gig thing. I was hooked.

Three: **The Third Track**

> *I'm gonna call her on the telephone*
> *Have her over 'cause I'm all alone*
> *I need excitement, oh I need it bad*
> *And it's the best I've had*

"Teenage Kicks" by The Undertones

THERE'S NOTHING BETTER than being up close to a band. You can see into their eyes. You can watch their interchanges and note that even the very best make mistakes. But getting a great position is often a major challenge. Over my gig-going years I've learnt some simple but effective gig tactics. This probably sounds a bit weird. What do you need gig tactics for? It's a concert. People play musical instruments. The audience watches. They applaud politely at the end of each track and when it's finished we all go home. *No.* That's the view of a non-muso. Gig-going is a fine art. One day the University of Music will have a degree in gig-going. Maybe they'll have my book in the reference section. I can but dream.

The point is quite basic. Too often at a gig you find yourself standing in the wrong place. Maybe you find yourself next to the drunken nutter, or Peter Crouch's taller brother stands plum in front of your line of vision. Typically, though, you can't move. You're hemmed in. The crowd are restless, eager to hear and see the band. The venue is filled with anticipation. The stage front is jammed and only those who are really pissed and shaped like some muscular ox get a pass through the obedient crowd to the front. So we normal folk have to wait.

What I've noticed with years of dedicated practice and fine-tuning is that, when track three is played, the crowd seems to calm down. Normally when a band comes on there's pandemonium that lasts for at least the first two tracks. Everyone is in the air. Pushing, pulling, jumping and screaming. But as track three eases out of the speakers, there's a slight lull. By now the band has settled down after their opening nerves and is moving nicely into the rhythm of the event. The crowd's sudden release of energy dissipates and there is some order, and – rather biblically – stillness prevails.

It's at this point that you make your move. As you're now free from the opening battering, you can head to the best spot you had craftily eyed up before and stay there for the rest of the show. You can get into the mosh pit or, if really determined, head down to the front row. In my early years there weren't barriers separating the crowd from the stage. We could actually get to the front and lean on the stage itself. With a good stretch you could touch the lead singer's grubby boots. If smart you'd put your jumper or beer neatly behind the back of the monitor. We even used to climb on stage with the bands. Today it's all metal barriers and security guys with bright ear protectors.

This Third Track move has always worked for me. I use it at virtually every gig if I get that urge to be close and intimate. Of course, this is subject to who is playing. It isn't very effective at an all-seated acoustic gig, I've found. Waiting until track three ends and then running insanely from row C to the stage doesn't go down well. In fact you're more likely to be asked to leave by the performer rather than security if you try this, so be warned.

Over the years, an experienced gig-goer develops a real armoury of tricks to get to the best spot in the house. I recall at the recent Specials reunion how effective the Third Track trick came off. I have to admit that this tactical manoeuvre is significantly helped by age. The Specials are a class act. They, with the other two-tone bands like Madness, The Selecter and The Beat, created a generation of musos and a range of ageless hits. So it was with huge excitement that friends Stu, Steve and I popped down to the Brixton Academy to see them on their famous reunion tour in 2007. Ok, it wasn't the full line-up. Jerry Dammers had apparently not made it up with Terry Hall. However, the rest of the crew had, and they were back on tour… like so many other 1980s bands.

Our pre-gig meet in the nearby pub supplied us with enough quality beer not to have to endure the expensive bland brands served at the otherwise magnificent Brixton Academy. After the security frisk we headed to the front and found ourselves in a good position to the right of the stage but quite a few rows back.

The crowd were very excitable, with a real cross-section of musos. There was a good atmosphere. The Academy was buzzing with pre-event banter and chitty-chat. People were smiling and engaging in millions of conversations. Some of the audience hadn't seen The Specials since 1982. Looking around, there were many who probably weren't born the last time this band played live. But together we all eagerly waited for them to emerge on to the stage.

Typically late and after plenty of catcalling from the now slightly over-excited and impatient crowd, the house lights dropped and Terry and crew emerged from the back of the stage. The crowd screamed and cheered. The first track was "Do the Dog" and the place exploded. Everyone was jumping, many were pushing and shoving. Latecomers charged from the back and it was pretty manic. The second track was "Dawning of a New Era" and still everyone was jumping mad. By now we had the vibe and knew we were in for a very special evening. The sound was loud and everyone was singing if not screaming along. We, though, were still a few rows from the front but feeling the urge to get close.

Next up was "Gangsters" and then Terry slowed things down. Time to catch breath. The crowd seemed to pull back from the stage… those at the front seemed to have expended their energy. Now was my chance and I went for it. As the majority rocked backwards I moved forward. This is what I call the Third Track parting. Virtually on cue, as always at the rockier gigs, the calm descended.

Terry picked up the mic again and I opened my eyes. There I was, standing in row two. Brilliant. I'm right at the front of stage. Slap in the centre. I could read the set list even though it was up-side down. I know people who'd sell their record collection to be here. The rest of the night was spent protecting row one as the mad crowd bashed into my back. But I didn't care. I was right at the front. I could almost touch Terry's laces. This is all part of the package. Stu and Steve were somewhere in the mayhem behind me. I couldn't see them and, rather selfishly, I didn't care. This was survival; each to their own. They would be fine.

In front of a huge black backcloth bearing their name in huge white letters, The Specials performed a tremendous set covering all their hits and many more. I was very close to putting this into my Top Ten of gigs. Certainly top twenty. We were lucky, though, because The Specials on this long overdue reunion had had to cancel their first night. Terry apologised as he had got ill and blamed it on the football. He then proceeded to boast about his beloved Man United beating Arsenal in the Champions League, which received a mixed response from this London audience. In an attempt to demonstrate his football prowess he brought out a football and then unleashed his right foot. But Terry is a musician and not Giggsy. His shot slammed into the monitor in front of him and spun up in the air and into the crowd behind me.

The show continued; hit after hit was masterfully performed to us. "Friday Night Saturday Morning" was my standout track, and for days I wouldn't stop singing it. With a short encore consisting of "Too Much Too Young," "Skinhead Moonstomp" and ending with "Enjoy Yourself," that was it. The house lights were on. The crowd started to disperse… sweaty, tired but very well entertained and still singing the classic anthem track "Enjoy Yourself."

I found Stu only a few feet away. He said that Jonathan Ross had been next to him but retired early saying he was too old for this. We agreed in unison that it was an excellent show. Steve then appeared and he said the same.

Then I noticed something.

'Steve, what's with the jumper thing?' I enquired, staring at his rather protruding stomach. Speechlessly and slowly, he lifted his shirt and displayed majestically the football 'our Terry' had miscued. What a night!

Four: **Verse Four**

> *Every time just like the last*
> *On her ship tied to the mast*
> *To distant lands*
> *Takes both my hands*
> *Never a frown with golden brown*

"Golden Brown" by The Stranglers

LISTENING TO MUSIC IS FINE. Seeing it played live and raw is even better. There is, though, an even bigger buzz, and that is to actually play music live *yourself*. To be in a band. Many of the bands I've grown to love and adore over the years were formed in untidy bedrooms, probably with dads and mums rushing out to visit people they never knew or banging on the ceiling from the floor below, screaming 'Keep the noise down!'

You hear stories of so many kids, locking themselves in said untidy rooms for days, months, years, strumming away to their favourite bands. All madly dreaming that, one day, they too will have a hit album, a record contract, groupies, wild sex, drugs *and* rock 'n' roll. For many, the dream fades quickly when the first guitar string snaps and dad says 'fix it yourself,' or when your hand just can't make a G minor 7th chord.

School is a good place to start, and so many have done. John Lennon first talked to George Harrison on the bus to school. Bono and The Edge met at high school… the list goes on. It was at my school that I met a few guys who also enjoyed music – not necessarily the same tastes as me, but at least they had also found – for their own personal reasons – that same lust and desire to create their own raw sound.

My first instrument was the drums. It was an easy way to start playing music and it gave me quick access to making my own live music. Drummers are different. They have an image of being the maverick, often the mad one – sometimes the recluse. A series of drummers have had a huge influence over me. John Bonham from Led Zeppelin and Keith Moon from The Who are two of my all-time heroes. These madmen, I thought, held it all together without having to learn complex stuff like music sheets. They gave the impression that all they had to do was sit at the back smashing away, keeping everything in time and to a rhythm. It isn't that simple – though the best drummers make it sound that way. The rawness of John Bonham's drumming, the sheer strength, the variety and heavy bass drum made his playing somehow stand out for me.

I've always thought that drums are the backbone to real rock music. Classic tracks such as "Won't Get Fooled Again" by The Who, "Ace of Spades" by Motorhead and "In My Time of Dying" by Led Zeppelin wouldn't have the same power and energy without that solid drum beat behind the dominant guitar and screaming vocal.

I probably took up the drums as a result of one – if not *the* – greatest musical disappointment of my early years: not going to piano lessons. I'll never forget that cold dark evening in late autumn. Taking after my mum, I had started to show some interest in music. In fact we had a piano, which my grandmother would play when she came down to stay. I was drawn to her as she played stuff I had never heard; more to the point I thought most of it, due to her hearing problem, was out of tune. I never said anything. I would simply clap politely at the end.

I rarely heard my mum play when I was a child, although I do now. When we visit my parents we usually persuade the children to encourage her to give a short performance. Full credit to someone normally quite shy and reserved that she can revel in the attention.

So back in the late 1970s I must have declared an interest in learning to play. Dutifully, my mum went on the search for a tutor. The tutor must have been reasonably close as we didn't have a car and buses were… well, enough said.

When the big day – rather evening – arrived, something popped. I bottled it. I said, in a pitiful way, a sad way, 'I don't want to go.' I wasn't proud but I've never really understood why

I couldn't face going. Surely this would have been the time for parents to make demands on their child, a time to say, 'come on, son, give it one go… I'm sure you'll like it… Look, we have a commitment… get your arse away from the TV, you *are* going.'

No. Mum said, 'Are you sure?' No questions as to why. No threat of pocket money deduction or the lost opportunity to play for the London Symphony Orchestra. She picked up the phone, called the teacher and said that I wouldn't be the teacher's destiny child.

I just went back to watching TV… maybe it was a good episode of *Scooby-Doo*?

It took me over ten years to say to my mum I'd like to learn a musical instrument. Notably I always addressed this question to my mum. My dad liked music, classical. Beethoven and Strauss. To be fair he took mum and me to see classical performances. I vividly remember seeing some famous performance at the Royal Festival Hall. A very posh place. You had to be there and seated on time, and you also had to clap at the right times. I remember being at one event ready to start the applause when a strong firm hand reached over and rested on mine. It wasn't the time to applaud. I was saved from heaping embarrassment and shame on the family in front of the rich and famous of the day.

I always recall that image every time I go back to the Royal Festival Hall… that concrete monstrosity. Even on my first visit I thought what a horrible building. It's all concrete, cold and very uninviting. 'Where are the bricks?' I'd ask myself. Everything at that time seemed hard, rough and plain. Maybe I was starting to show an early interest in planning and urban design. The buildings, I felt, rather summed up the music at this time. We needed something new and my God did we get it… by 1976 we had punk and my world of music simply exploded.

It wasn't until 1984 that I returned to the Royal Festival Hall. This time it wasn't to hear a lovely Viennese waltz or a piano concerto in D minor but to hear the beautifully seductive vocals of Elizabeth (Liz) Fraser. Liz was the wonderfully *avant-garde* singer in Cocteau Twins. Cocteau Twins were unique in so many ways. It wasn't just their rich haunting guitars and slow beat supported by eloquent vocals, it was *everything*: the packaging, the artwork and the kind of bizarre 4AD record label created by Ivo Watts-Russell and Peter Kent. I fell in love with Cocteau Twins the first time I heard them. I was learning to print photographs in a small studio off the Cowley Road in Oxford. There I was, deep in the darkroom, shifting my would-be works of art from tray to tray when this wonderfully haunting, slightly repetitive but ethereal sound rained down.

'Who on earth are you playing?' I excitedly asked the guy who ran the studio.

'Cocteau Twins,' he said slightly, with the air that they were as famous as The Who.

'The Cocktail Twins,' I wrongly repeated.

'No, Cocteau Twins. There's no *The*. And it's *Cocteau*,' he replied knowledgeably.

That was it. I pulled my prints out of the tray to dry and ran off to Our Price and bought the album. I must have played it non-stop for the whole term; certainly by Christmas everyone at Oxford Poly had heard about them.

The wonderful thing about being a unique and slightly distant indie band was that they didn't play many gigs. It was a tricky sound to perform live. They needed lots of backing tracks, samples and a drum machine. When they did play they would avoid the obvious Hammy Odeon and Town and Country Club. So there I was in the same venue as I had been in when I was 13, waiting eagerly for Liz, Simon and Robin to emerge on stage.

What was also brilliant was that the same RFH stewards were on duty. I mean, the stewards were smartly attired older men in red jackets, carefully checking the tickets of hundreds of punks, Mohicans, Goths and untrendy students. Most of the crowd must have thought they were on another planet… getting shown to your seat. It was a precious evening and Liz was brilliant.

But back to drums. So at the delicate age of 15 I decided the time was right to learn to play. I wanted to be in a band. I know it wasn't about being rich and famous. I simply wanted a new tool in my personal repertoire. I wanted to make music. I didn't necessarily want to write stuff but that would have been good. I just wanted to play.

As I look back, the drums were the heart and engine room of the band. They seemed louder to me than other instruments. I seemed to hear the drums over everything else. They were the obvious instrument for a young growing boy to stretch out and become a man. John Bonham especially, amongst all the powering guitars and high-pitched vocals, jumped across his Pearl kit and grabbed me by the throat.

My school had a music block. It was a smart though rather boring-looking building with an indoor auditorium. I remember one day walking past the small rooms at the front of the building and seeing a white drum kit sitting alone, no one on it. It must have touched a nerve. John Bonham smashed his way into my tiny mind with a huge Zeppelin track and my head went crashing through the Paiste cymbals. That was it. I was going to learn to play the drums. All I had to do was ask mum if I could.

Mum was fine. Dad was silent. It turned out later he wasn't keen… he obviously had plans for me but never let on. I think he was worried his one and only son would fall into disrepute and take off into the arty world full of drugs, sex and rock 'n' roll. He wanted me to have a good steady job and that was why I was at some rather posh school in the middle of nowhere, paid for by his very hard work. I can see why he was silent.

But with mum's approval, and no doubt an off-the-record, behind-the-scenes conversation between my parents, I was allowed to sign up. My teacher was the jazz session drummer Bill Castle. He was very good. He made it seem all very natural and easy. I learnt quickly that this playing thing would need a bit of input from me. This shook me up as I wasn't the smartest in class; in fact I was probably one of the most educationally challenged in that posh place. I was late in discovering the reason for learning, and what it means when you've done it. I sometimes thought that if Bradfield had been in Essex, Ian Dury (as teacher) would have written a song about me. Then again, reading his story, while I respect him I'm sure we wouldn't have got on.

Through the drums I found a purpose. I was determined to learn. I'd spend hours sitting on the floor, in fact any floor, with a couple of sticks practising rhythms.

It was always cool at school to be in a band. Being in a band had all the clichés. Girl-pulling power, street cred with mates, getting talked about over lunch, being stared at and the odd smile from the juniors. But that wasn't our intention, nor was it about making the next hit record and starting a rock 'n' roll career. We were simply a few mates who wanted to play live music.

After a few personnel changes, our four-piece consisted of Mr

James Handford, lead guitar and vocals; on bass we had Charlie Tincknell – besides being a great goalkeeper, he was a solid bass player, even though he was learning lead guitar; on keyboard was Rick Tyler – Jim and he were the brains and lead musicians. I was the drummer. I had the easy job – hit the drum skins in a rather timely way and create some form of rhythm while keeping time.

One spring holiday we all decamped to Jim's house where we set up an improvised studio. I loved Jim's house. It was in the middle of nowhere. It was a picture postcard English cottage. A central door surrounded by climbing roses and honeysuckle. Inside it had the wonderful smell of lovely winter wood fires. We used to make up haunting ghost stories about a burning house and people being stuck in upstairs windows. How dramatic.

In the living room we set up the kit and equipment and then sat down. Now, most bands had a style and a theme already sorted. They knew what to do. Someone would have a bag full of score sheets and between them they'd select a few and get going. We didn't, we just sat staring at each other.

'So, what are we playing then?' I piped up. There was a long silence.

'Ah… how about The Stranglers?' Rick suggested after a minute of reflective thought.

'Ok, which one?' I enquired supportively. There was more deafening silence as we all deliberated.

'What about "Peaches"? That's a great track,' I added.

'I'm not sure of the chords,' Charlie called out.

'Well they can't be that hard. It's The Stranglers, not Stravinsky,' I muttered.

'"Golden Brown?"' Jim called out in inspiration. Everyone looked at each other. No dissent. So it was agreed. "Golden Brown" would be our first track.

And with that we started pulling it together. Of course there are plenty of easier tracks to pick. "Golden Brown" is a magnificent track but it's also complex, and changes rhythm from the typical four-four to an impressive seven-eight. We weren't put off and managed to create our own, slightly simpler version.

After a couple of days we managed to pull a short set list together. These were mostly covers but we also managed to pen two new tunes. These were written by Rick. This would give us some respectability and, hopefully, interest. With a reasonable set list in hand and tracks we could all play, we still didn't have a band name. After another practice session we went for a walk.

Jim's house was in a remote part of Hampshire. It wasn't even in a village. The long lanes were archetypally English. It was a wonderful day, warm and bright. The hedged lane meandered to a small church – as musicians looking for inspiration we went in. The church was cool inside. Its white stone walls created a lovely bright natural light. As bands do, apparently, we just mooched around. I say that without any full knowledge whatsoever of what a real band does when not playing. I had never been in a band but this was the image portrayed by many of the New Wave acts storming the charts. I picked up a Bible and suggested, 'how about 'The Bible'?'

'No that doesn't work,' said Rick. (*How wrong we were – there was a well-respected band from Cambridge who took it up. They were fronted by Boo Hewerdine, whom I got to know a bit few years later after I have made my move from Oxford in 1987*).

We still didn't have a name. Getting slightly desperate I picked up the Bible again. 'How about 'The Verse'? 'Verse Three'? No. There are four of us. 'Verse Four'? That's it, 'Verse Four''.

'Yep. That's good. It works!' agreed a weary set of youth.

So with that we became Verse Four. We were now a real band. We had a set of songs we could play, and now a name. A rather good one I felt. Shame about 'The Bible' but I think Boo and crew deserved it much more than we did. I've never asked them where they got their name from – I will one day.

By the end of three days of rehearsals and getting a bit drunk we were ready. We already had two gigs lined up. Our first gig was in a few days' time at a friend's house party, hence the urgency to learn a few tracks and get a band name.

ERD the car was now becoming quite famous and very useful. On the evening of the party we packed in the gear and drove off to some place I'd never heard of and will never remember. The house was one of those large family houses you find in the country. Large drive, walled garden with perfect striped lawn and meticulously maintained shrubberies. We were greeted with smiles and directed to a stage. Well it wasn't exactly a stage, just a small side room off the main lounge area. Here we set up our kit and, once we were ready, did that gig thing of practising a couple of tracks. We did our own soundcheck. We then went off and got some food and a beer. I don't recall being scared. A bit nervous, yes, but the adrenaline hadn't kicked in and we were nicely settled after downing more beers.

Then we were on. Jim led us on to the stage. Ok, the small room area. The set list was agreed and after a countdown of, 'one, two, three, four…' from me, we were off.

I would love to boast that we played a stage-blowing stormer. And that after the set we were signed by Virgin and – before we could even print our first album sleeve – invited to the famous Abbey Road recording studios to lay down the tracks for our debut single while drinking champagne and pushing the totty away.

I thought we played ok. I did drop my sticks but only once. At least at one point everyone was watching. It was about midway through the set when everyone left. It was a bit soul-destroying playing to the empty room. I put it down to people being offered free booze and a live sex show next door. A few brave souls returned for our finale and we were given some cheers and applause at the end.

We half bowed to the small crowd and thanked them for listening. Rick, Charlie, Jim and I smiled slightly reticently. We weren't really sure what to make of it.

We grouped together and immediately hit the booze. It was a strange feeling. The nerves had transformed into excitement, which then became anxiety, which then turned into a feeling of being lost and confused. We had, though, played real live music, including some of our own stuff, to real people. We were officially, in my books, a real band. Verse Four were on the road and alive and well.

'Not a lot of people have done that,' I said to myself.

The party gig was our one and only rehearsal before our one and only paid show. I had managed to get the gig through a girl I used to see. I still don't know whether, in fact, we ever went out. She was sweet and we used to spend Sunday afternoons at my house snogging the tonsils out of each other. Her school was another posh place, St Mary's Convent, Ascot. A real, genuine, girls only school. Not a St Trinian's, but that didn't matter. It was too tightly controlled. Somehow Julie managed to get us a slot to play at an end of term party. I mentioned this to the other school band, who (to be honest) were much more punky than our rather reserved style. They were also louder and full of band bravado. They had experience, a longer set list *and* – although we never said it to them – they were better than us, so we agreed Verse Four would be the support act. Genuinely I can't remember their name. Oh well.

It would be tempting to say we had made it. Tonight we would play on a real stage, with some real lights and a largish crowd of screaming young girls. Fab. We arrived in good time and were shown a side room transformed into a dressing room. We shared this with our fellow band members and razzed away. The soundcheck went fine and I didn't drop a stick. Our dressing room was full of stage sets, stacked chairs, wooden tables. It wasn't really rock 'n' roll as we weren't allowed beer on the premises, so the rider consisted of a kettle, teabags and some cups for water. Hey, though, we weren't that fussed. The chance to play live to a real audience was enough for us.

Dead on time, which wasn't very rock 'n' roll, someone took hold of the microphone in the centre of the large stage and announced: 'Good evening! First on stage tonight is Verse Four.'

Rick, Jim, Charlie and I walked on to the stage. The room was a large school hall room typical of its time and purpose. Wooden panelling and floor with side bars for dance lessons. The stage was some four feet off the floor level, giving us height and visibility. The venue lights went out and we stumbled to our positions. The audience of some hundred St Mary's girls started screaming. We looked at each other in bemusement. It was surreal. We grinned and expected it all to disappear into a dream world. Suddenly we were getting a sliver, a taste of what it really must be like to be a rock star. For one minute in my life, I had more young girls screaming for me than Robbie Williams. Well, it was a nice dream. A short one.

Jim set us off and the crowd lapped it up. I was nervous. My role was to keep us all together, to keep solid time and add emphasis when necessary. It wasn't easy though. I had to dig deep to find some mental strength. By track three we were settled. The tension had gone. The party gig had done its trick and helped us to settle our nerves. All we could do now was to start to enjoy it.

Jim looked around and smiled. No sooner had we settled then Jim started to play the intro to our fourth track. The problem was that the track he started to play wasn't the next one on our set list.

He had missed one out. Somehow we all managed to regroup and switch songs. As the track closed, we all glared at each other. I think we pulled it off. The young convent pupils were singing and dancing, which was the only sign we needed.

We played our favourite home-made track, "No Martini in China." It was a slower number focussing on an electronic riff supported by a recurring guitar rhythm. It was a simple song with a nice vocal but it worked well and was certainly of the period. The crowd applauded and I sensed we all felt rewarded for being brave enough to try something new and our own.

Before we knew it, our short set came to an end. We had no more songs to play. The crowd were still cheering and waving. With a closing crash of cymbals we ended. I picked up my sticks, Jim and Charlie their guitars, and we walked off smiling and waving. Off stage we danced around madly while in the background we could still hear our audience cheering. We hugged each other in that manly bonding way. All we wanted to do was go back out there. The nervousness had pushed our adrenaline over the limit. We were on a real high.

Our pals, though, showed their experience and had the place screaming the walls down to The Clash's "London Calling." They put in an ace set and were well worth their headline role. At the end we all bonded and called the event a great success. I remember then going to collect the sixty quid from the very bemused schoolmistress, who looked down on us sternly. I don't think she enjoyed it. There wasn't any contract and we agreed to split the payment. Thirty quid each. For Verse Four this was our first and only ever payment. For the two gigs it had cost us about forty quid to hire some of our kit, so we made a financial loss. But emotionally and entertainment-wise we'd made a killing.

We packed the hired PA into ERD and headed home in silence. Each of us was lost in our moment of fame. We had, though, achieved an ambition. We had played live, survived and, in our own little way, felt like rock stars just for a few minutes. It would stay with us for a very, very long time.

Five: **Support Acts**

*Sometimes, when I look deep in your eyes,
I swear I can see your soul*

"Sometimes" by James

IS IT ME? I always thought a support band had one – but vital – role to play at a live gig: get the crowd worked up and excited. But, and this is the important bit, they mustn't overdo it. They mustn't, in any circumstances, work the crowd up so much that everyone comes away at the end singing their songs and shouting loudly, 'cor, I thought the support band was much better than the main act.'

But sometimes this *is* the case. I'm pleased to say that while I've watched many support acts over the years, not many have ever trumped the main act. There's this inbuilt respect thing. In return for that rare chance to perform in front of a large crowd you don't muck up. Play it down. Keep it steady. Be good but don't push it.

In reality this is probably because the headliner and their management select their support acts… with much care.

Of course bands have to start somewhere, so it's great to see many of my favourite acts actively encouraging local talent to be their support. Three cheers for them.

Along my gigging trip I've had the privilege of seeing some great support acts stepping out on their own. All were set on better things and becoming headliners in their own right.

One classic example was at Cambridge Corn Exchange in 1992, when Nottingham's Stereo MCs were billed to support Shaun Ryder's Happy Mondays. Lead singer Rob Birch and DJ partner Nick Hallam put in a pumping set. Within seconds and the first few bars of their rhythm-driven tracks, the expectant Cambridge crowd were all dancing madly as if given an electric shock. The powerful sound was so contagious that weeks later (in those days before downloading) I was still searching for some of their early back catalogue. Their performance was made even more memorable because this was a Sunday night and it was 'skool' the next day. Usually Sunday evening gigs are mellower affairs. The crowd are often subdued, having just recovered from Saturday night's hangover.

The Stereo MCs were rising stars. Formed in 1985, they were a band that had fought hard for recognition, apparently selling virtually everything they owned to put their message out and get noticed. By the early 1990s things were starting to pay off and they were invited to support the Happy Mondays, one of the most influential bands of the time.

Jez and I had discovered Stereo MCs in our usual random testing out of new sounds and bands. We were excited about a Sunday outing to see two quality bands of the time and deliberately took it easy the night before. We didn't want to ruin it.

It started so well. Immediately Rob had us swaying to his mesmeric vibe. Our hands and feet awoke, and before we knew it we were dancing. Arms were flying everywhere. The whole place was jumping around. We were in full flight. Each song got stronger and stronger. The climax was the brilliant "Connected" and "Step It Up." Wow! The band waved goodbye and we screamed back our approval. Awesome.

But that's when it all goes a bit Pete Tong. You see, maybe it was this Sunday thing but the Happy Mondays had obviously not travelled east before and clearly didn't own a map or satnav between them. Because by ten o'clock and over an hour after Rob and Nick had left the stage, we were still waiting for Shaun, Bez and the Madchester posse to appear… but I'll tell you more about this later on.

For me, Stereo MCs had been fabulous. They had simply not just stolen the show but also nicked all the drugs, booze and kit right under Ryder's nose. For all I cared, Bez could hang his tambourine on the peg of failure. Happy Mondays, like it or not, had simply been upstaged.

But luckily it wasn't always like that. In 1993 I managed to get tickets to see James play at the cosy UEA in Norwich. I love this small compact venue. It's such an intimate place. It isn't especially pretty and arguably not worthy of any architectural award, unless you like your architecture New Brutalist. Importantly at the UEA you can get really close to the stage and feel part of the gig. The main floor is set a few steps down and creates a mosh pit of its own. It's a tight venue, which allows great visibility of the stage from wherever you are.

Norwich in the early 1990s was a bit of a trek from new home in Cambridge by car, and impossible by public transport. My partner, soon to be wife, Jenny wasn't that keen when I politely suggested, 'come on, we have to go.'

'Why?'

'I want to see the support band.'

'Why?' she pestered.

'Because they're good,' I tentatively replied.

'But you haven't seen them before,' she correctly observed.

'I know. That's why I want to get there early. I want to see them… Oh please, just get in the car.' Swearing wasn't really an option, but slamming the door and driving off certainly was.

The good news is that we got to the UEA just in time. The support band came on just as we collected our drinks from the bar. The other good news was that they saved their one hit to date for later on. The one I had heard on the radio and had bought a nice seven-inch single from Parrot Records on King Street. The track was "Creep" and the band was Radiohead.

'See this band? They're going to be massive,' I said prophetically to Jen, who was still thinking, 'why on earth have we rushed all this way to hear *that*?' I could sense she wasn't impressed. It was written like a tattoo across the forehead – a huge question mark that on anyone else would say, 'what on earth was that?'

Well, I have to say that for once I was right. She has never liked them even though they went on to become a mega super group. Times like this make me smile. There I am, pursuing my passion… the love of my life devotedly tags along to a gig she doesn't enjoy – and all I can do is make a stubborn remark. What's that book called? *Men Are from Mars, Women Are from Venus*? It's quite solitary, this gigging lark.

James, I'm pleased to report, were also excellent. While Radiohead were artistic and cloudy, James were down-to-earth, jovial and party-like. Radiohead offered intrigue and were hard to fathom, while Tim Booth and crew were full-on crowd pleasers. Both bands complemented each other. As we travelled through the James set list, the crowd became louder and louder. I looked around the mixed crowd of musos and students. Everyone was smiling and singing. Everyone was having a ball. We ended a brilliant evening singing "Born of Frustration" and "Sit Down." Wonderful!

Promoting bands has taken various forms and approaches over the years. In the mid-1980s and 1990s some record labels put on tours to promote their up-and-coming bands to widen their appeal and spread their sound. We were lucky in some ways that Cambridge Corn Exchange was often used as such a venue. This was made even better when my mate Nic's ex-girlfriend Nicki landed an A&R job for a small indie promoter. Without asking, she very kindly added me on to their mailing list. As a result I kept the postman busy, receiving numerous new releases to comment on. For years I was regarded in London as some top DJ playing new tunes to the masses of rural Cambridge. I did do the odd event but the audience wasn't really a fair representation of the discerning local music population. But who cared? I had become a regular reviewer and they, apparently, loved my fair, open and honest commentary on loads of new acts. I was careful not to really slag anyone off just in case they turned out to be the new U2.

Two bands being massively plugged at this time were The Verve and Smashing Pumpkins. I had heard a few tracks from both and liked them. The Pumpkins had an edge and great guitar sound which resonated well with me. So I was delighted to hear the A&R crew say, 'yes, of course you can have tickets… you're on the guest list!'

'Brill!' I replied.

The VIP section at the Cambridge Corn Exchange is a mezzanine floor under the main seated area at the back of the hall. It's a bit claustrophobic and some distance from the stage. But you shouldn't grumble if you're an invited guest. It was also rather timely as I was recovering from a Gazza – no, not a mega dentist-chair session – but the reconstruction of my anterior cruciate ligament. If you play footy you'll know this is the injury of all injuries. It bloody hurts, makes one of the worst sounds out there and takes a long time to recover from. The morphine was good though. Anyhow, I needed to rest my leg, which was still tightly wrapped, so being out of the crowd for this gig was sensible.

The special bonus was that there were real VIPs in this section that night. In fact one of them had most of his family there. While moving gingerly around on my crutches, I had one of those difficult moments. In front of me was the one and only legendary John Peel. He was with the Pig – if you aren't up with the beat this was the rather unaffectionate term he used for his wife – and a couple of the Peel offspring on a day out from Peel Acres down in Suffolk. I looked up, and for what must have been ages I managed to muster just one word.

'Hello,' I said wimpishly.

John smiled back and sat down.

'*You dick!*' I screamed to myself. There you are, in the VIP section of a gig, with John Peel and his family. John bloody Peel, you knob. Ok, I'm sure he doesn't want to be disturbed but I could've asked an intelligent or witty question, such as whether he thought 'Richard Ashcroft is destined to be the new Paul McCartney,' or if 'James Ida from the Pumpkins is the key to their musical genius.' But no. All I could muster was a pathetic 'hello.'

I'm pleased to say both bands provided a great show and went on to much better things. And as a PR event it worked well. Arguably, this was an evening of two support acts. Two bands that would in fact go on to achieve huge status and acclaim. However, my overall enjoyment was haunted by a missed chance to speak to a musical genius. A man who has helped so many of my favourite bands to expose their musical prowess to world and reap huge success. A lost opportunity, and one I have to live with.

Of course, as I said earlier, the purpose of the support act is to liven up the crowd without taking over. If anyone could do it and do it in style then it was Status Quo. The Quo, love 'em or hate 'em, have cornered the market in making so much from a simple but very clever set of rock 'n' roll chords. In 1986, Queen were booked to play at the old Wembley – or, as us footy nutters would say, *Wemberley* – Stadium. The event included INXS, who opened the event. They played a good solid set and Hutchence clearly milked the opportunity to woo the crowd.

Next up were The Quo. They entered the vast stage with a determination to Rock All Over the World… and they damn well nearly did it. Whether it was the weather, the beer… Quo played a stormer. Everyone in the packed stadium crowd were banging their heads as Francis Rossi and Rick Parfitt pounded the stage. It was a blinder and you couldn't hold back on demanding more. I moved close to the stage, pulled nearer by their brilliance.

Queen, fronted by the ultimate lead singer, the unique Freddie Mercury, were admittedly brilliant. (Check out the live album of this gig.) There aren't many performers in the world who have not only the charisma but also the voice to knock down a whole stadium. Freddie was born to perform. He had that amazing gift of being able to grab everyone's attention by his stage presence and, ultimately, some of the most brilliant vocals ever. Perhaps some of the exotic spice of his birthplace, Zanzibar, had seeped into his bloodstream.

The Quo set had got me really close to the stage. There was a tense atmosphere down the front. I recall quite a few fights breaking out. The event seemed to have attracted a number of small gangs who weren't really interested in the music. It was the era of aggro, and tonight there was plenty of it.

I turned my attention to the front. Freddie was on fire. He came on stage dressed as the Queen, fully kitted out in a bright red robe and crown. He quickly shed these and, now in his brilliant yellow jacket and white vest, spent most of the show prancing around the stage and gripping the mic stand like a devoted lover. He regularly took up the Freddie pose – mic stand held high, neck and head bent backwards, screaming. Brilliant! The pure balls of the man. The crowd, now wonderfully wound up by Quo, were in full voice. Every note Freddie sang, we sang back. We entered into a singing challenge half way through the set. Freddie's mindblowing *a cappella* – a race through the vocal scales that left most of us hoarse by the end – raised the bar. He won by miles. Freddie is a huge loss to the music scene, even today. At least he left a real legacy behind. The show closed with the thunderous "God Save the Queen," everyone in this huge iconic stadium singing as one. On the way to the tube it was hard not to join in the instantaneous classics such as "Bicycle Race" and "We Are the Champions."

Quo had rocked us hard but Queen left the echo.

I have to admit that on occasions I've not been very supportive when it comes to support acts. I admit this is truly awful. My pathetic excuse is that at my time of life other pressures mean that the priority has to be to see the main act. If, however, I can sneak in the support that's a bonus, especially if I've heard of them and my interest is sufficiently aroused.

Recently, I managed to wangle a sneaky trip to Birmingham to see the wonderful Florence and the Machine. I like Florence. She has an amazing voice, with the kind of face that radiates loving, caring and genuineness. This gig, on 13 March 2012, was out at the LG Arena – that wonderful, intimate, personally named venue (I mock), part of the NEC in Birmingham.

But the real draw was the chance to see a band I had stumbled across on the *Later with Jools* programme. This show has become that one place on telly where musos can now hear classic artists, together with the new and up-and-coming stars. Sadly for me, and a variety of pathetic reasons, I don't get to see Jools' show very often. But one night in the autumn of 2011 I caught up with him. I had been out at a gig and was up for more music. The show had some great new acts. It included a brilliant Lana Del Rey, Ghostpoet and a band that made me go, 'wow, I like *them*.' They were The Horrors, a band from Southend-on-Sea who were plugging their second album.

I'm sure I'm not alone, but it's rare that you suddenly hear a song or band and go, 'fab… that's interesting. Who's that? That's a sound I've been waiting for.' Now, The Horrors have plenty of influences, and I reckon many are from my early years in muso-land. But what's wonderful is that they grab these varied styles, rhythms and riffs, and blend them into something completely their own. They make it all work in a new and exciting way. So when I heard The Horrors were supporting Florence I thought 'yep, this is a must-go gig.' I managed to get a standing ticket for this sold-out gig through Emily on eBay. Ta.

I rushed into the huge boring hangar at the NEC just as The Horrors entered the huge, daunting stage. I feel for support bands in such large venues. Besides the horrid echo and distortion, there's the problem of the crowd. Most of those present simply aren't interested in anything but getting in loads of beer before the main act appears. Support bands often face gig-goers feeling disenfranchised, sometimes turning hostile. Luckily, tonight the early crowd were receptive and compassionate. This was probably because most of the audience were female. Girls have that rare quality of being fair-minded and empathic – unless of course, they're filled with vodka and Red Bull.

Tonight, with a large crowd already settled in their tiered seats or standing areas, The Horrors gave a grand performance. As they went through their set, more and more hands were raised applauding a gutsy show. It was also great to see a band appear settled and confident. The Horrors offer something different. Maybe it's a rehash of the 1980s but they pull it off well. Their set ended with the calming and indulgent "Still Life."

The Horrors set us up nicely for a terrific show from a confident and determined Florence. Florence pulled off a great gig. Supported by a brilliant band and backing singers, she regularly smiled between those stretching vocals and was obviously comfortable with this crowd.

Sometimes you need to step outside your comfort zone. It's all too easy just to sit back and not bother. So much nowadays is all on a plate… Well, it feels that way. But musos know that on this journey you need to get out and experiment.

Experimentation requires risk-taking. For a real muso it means taking a punt. A long-odds bet. It means tipping the nag that even the tic-tac man has never heard of.

The other day, Nic spotted a gig my radar had missed. It featured one of my favourite trance bands, Banco de Gaia, supporting the respected System 7.

Now, I love Banco de Gaia. For me they make Glastonbury. Toby Marks has created that perfect soundtrack for the restless traveller, epitomised by his *Last Train to Lhasa* album – it takes you on a moving but mystical journey across the beautiful Himalayas into a distant world, millions of miles away in time and culture.

The gig was at The Garage, near Highbury and Islington tube station in London. It's a compact venue that allows easy access to the stage and plenty of space to move around. You can get really close. Nic and I agreed that it matched our criteria for a good venue.

We arrived early to get into the trance vibe and were nicely entertained by DJ Aliji, who perfectly whetted our appetite. Now, not knowing the headliner System 7, I started to pay attention to what was the most eclectic of audiences. It got me reminiscing.

Isn't it fascinating how varied an audience can be? Here we are, complete strangers, drawn together by interest, love or even passion for a bunch of musically talented folk who are standing on stage in front of us, waiting to play their stuff and at the same time play with our emotion and heartstrings. Tonight, as I looked around, it triggered a flashback. I could see the faces of some of the many people I've had the privilege to have met over my gig-going years.

Let me introduce a few of them to you.

First there was Dave. He was a taxi driver. To be honest he was slightly overweight but seemed comfortable wearing a light patterned Fred Perry short-sleeved shirt, baggy shorts (with those large combat-style pockets to reduce the reality of his protruding belly) and white plimsolls. He loved two-tone music but also reggae. We met at The Specials reunion gig at Brixton. He first saw them in 1982.

I met Kevin at a mad and loud festival. He was well coiffured, with a multi-coloured open shirt covering a white T-shirt with some childishly drawn face on it. He seemed never to stop smiling. I bet myself that he looked the same now as he did when he went to his first party in 1968 and took LSD. He loved trance and reggae. We chatted away before the early evening DJ set. He was the one who casually started things up. We shared a small spliff.

I met Charlotte, who preferred to be known as Charlie, at another slightly quieter festival. She lived for travelling, and recounted endless stories of how she bathed on the very beach in Thailand which was used in the famous film set. She worked out, and her white shirt showed off her well-formed bronzed biceps, which carried a small, faded tattoo on her shoulder. She told me how she loved yoga and live music. Her happy smile summed it up.

Many gig-goers are couples. In the mid-1990s I met some real movers, Chrissie and Martin, at a small folky gig. Chrissie was a Sixties' child from the Somerset countryside. She was proud she grew up on real cider. We joked about early partners and passionate embraces in the meadow by the burbling stream. For some bizarre reason she boasted about her divorce and that she now made lavender bags in her wild garden. Martin, her new partner, was more hairy than the Hairy Bikers. He had known Chrissie since primary school but wasn't her first love. As the band came on stage Chrissie took off, dancing with arms flailing like on her wedding night, while Martin and I stood with our hands in our pockets. I recall we wiggled our hips. We all smiled. Everyone was smiling.

I remember sitting down for a sumptuous Moroccan tagine at Glastonbury a few years ago with Sarah. We'd just seen the gorgeous Katie Melua. Hungrily, we tucked into the superb food and got talking to a young man. He was chatty and pleasant. We exchanged thoughts on the festival and the lovely food.

'Are you having a good festival?' we asked this young man with a small beard.

'Sure. It's such a great place.'

We all agreed it was a unique event and for once we'd been lucky with the weather.

'Who have you enjoyed?' we asked.

'I haven't seen many acts. Actually I've been performing,' he replied.

'What do you play?' I asked with genuine interest.

'Oh, I'm a beat boxer.'

'Ok,' I said, thinking hard.

'I'm Beardyman,' he replied. After we'd said our goodbyes, good luck and *bonnes chances* I explained proudly to Sarah who this young man was. 'Oh,' she said nonchalantly. Well, *I* was impressed.

Back at the gig, I come out of my daydream and look around at the medley of audience stars. Young, old, hippies, rockers, girls, bald men. Everyone was smiling. Nic and I had had a shit day but now we could smile too.

Banco de Gaia played a lovely trance set with a seamless video about journeying all over the wonderful Far East. Teasing us about our past adventures, it seduced us to do more while reminding us of how these places are so poor in cash but so rich in mind. It was superb to look at, and reminded me that there's something so special about music, and it only gets better when you venture out and see it live.

The lack of a status battle between the support and main act epitomised the beauty of this event. Everyone was in it together. The bands wanted to play; we, the eclectic audience from all over, simply wanted to smile, dance and be entertained. As a tonic and reality check on life, this was it. We came away so much brighter than when we had entered. Brilliant. I felt better.

Six: **Festivals**

The first time ever I saw your face
I thought the sun rose in your eyes
And the moon and the stars were the gifts you gave
To the dark and the endless skies, my love

"The First Time Ever" by Roberta Flack

'YOU NEED TO BRING A NEW TENT,' said Keith on the phone.
　'What?' I queried.
　'Your tent is broken. You need to get another one,' he argued in his soft scouse accent.
　'Ha ha ha, very funny.' I cackled.
　'No, I'm serious. Your tent is broken. Someone fell on it last night and snapped the main pole. Get yourself another one.'
　Keith, I now realised, was probably not joking. I had the choice of risk it or play safe. So to be on the safe side, I popped into the large supermarket just off junction 12 of the M4 and bought myself a neat four-man tent. It was green, of course, and soon I was back en route to my annual pilgrimage to another festival.
　Festivals are very special events for me. There were apparently over seven hundred festivals in the UK alone in 2010. Seven hundred. That's two a day throughout the year – amazing! The great thing about festivals today is the vast range of styles and themes. There's one for just about everybody. From the hardcore metal events such as Download and Bloodstock to the sedate entertainment for all the family at Hop Farm and Cornbury. There's even a retro event called Vintage.
　I'd like to think that everyone who has been to a gig has, at some stage in their lives, braved up and attended a full-on festival.

I'm not talking about a one-day event, that's just a long gig. It doesn't really matter which one you go to. It's the whole shebang that's important. You see, while gigs offer so much, they're like any album, restricted by time. At most normal gigs you can expect anything from an hour to a three-hour show. But at a festival we're talking days. Of course, given this extension of time it offers you space to experiment. The chance to really immerse yourself. With the bigger physical space and extra minutes comes the chance to see anything from your favourite to the most obscure, depending on who's on the bill.

Festivals are also a meteorological gamble, especially those in the UK. Everyone knows that we Brits are famed for talking about the weather, and so when it comes to a festival, in terms of comfort and joy we're playing a game of Russian roulette. While I've enjoyed the ecstasy of being bathed in glorious sunshine, I've also been drowned in mud baths with fellow punters, subjected to an ordeal more demanding than *I'm a Celebrity Get Me Out of Here* or a long weekend on the Aldershot special services assault course. I can see why festivals, while popular, are not everyone's cup of chai.

It's the range and vast amount of music – all in one place, with the freedom to do and see what you like – that's the main draw for me. Where on earth can you see 30 bands over 72 hours? Where can you see the new and upcoming genius followed by the classic mega band?

But festivals are more than the music. Amongst the mud, straw and huge stages you can find space and the opportunity to meet up with friends, to share (not literally) a portaloo, rummage for soggy bog roll in a mud-splattered rucksack. You can also witness things only seen in films. Watch grown dads flouncing around in their wife's wedding dress or stare at someone brave enough to wear a bright green mankini. A place where you can get snogged by strangers and not have to buy them dinner or end up laughing your FatFace socks off as your best friend slips up in a mud bath while carrying his round of watered-down lager. Festivals are bloody good fun.

I went to my first festival when I was 16. My first was the famous Reading Rock Festival. Through rain and shine it's still going strong. Back in the 1970s it was a real rock festival, and I mean *rock* festival, even though it was titled the National Jazz and Blues Festival. Growing up nearby, my childhood impression was that it was a biker's heaven: a mecca of jeans and denim, a palace of ripped leather jackets with Harley Davidson emblems on the back. There were even Hells Angels at the sides of the stage. It was true. I saw them. In the late 1970s my Reading became a *rock* capital –indie, dance, techno and drum 'n' bass were just glints in a future musician's eye.

Even by 1980, Reading Rock, as it had become known, had been on the festival scene or circuit (in muso-speak) for a number of years. It also had the unique advantage over any other festival in the UK in that it was walkable from my house. So when my cousin David came over on that August Bank Holiday for one of those sombre Sunday lunches where the rellies gossiped and the kids were told to play nicely, it was joy to hear him suggest that maybe he and I should go to the festival. It was even better because he had a car and we didn't have to trudge across Prospect Park.

Reading Rock was an established rock festival with a huge rock reputation. And this was reflected in the audience – simply the best collective of old, new and ancient hippy rockers who delighted in the opportunity of getting covered in mud and totally slammed on real cider and any form of ale. No one ever thought of washing – the dream was a day's headbanging to the top rock bands of the decade. Black leather and denim were the dress code, plus plenty of mud to show that you hadn't, like David and me, just turned up for the one day. It was also overtly tribal. Even though punk had emerged as a serious new musical style by this time, this was not a place to bring your swastika T-shirt or coloured hair. Reading Rock was beer, smells, dirt, long hair, black leather, ripped blue denim and loud guitars.

I learnt while writing this book that in 1979 there had been so much violence between all the rockers, punks, skinheads and New Wave followers who had come to see their various bands that the promoters decided to focus on heavy rock and metal the next year, which was my first visit: Sunday, 24 August 1980.

Reading Rock takes place in a so-called meadow a mile or so out of town to the west, next to the River Thames – the river where happy smiling boaters play at being Three Men in a Boat and where pleasure cruisers travel upstream to the quintessentially English villages of Pangbourne, Streatley and Goring. Now, on a usual Sunday this must be a wonderful experience, watching the world float past and having the chance to stare into the back gardens of the rich and filthy rich. But the scene dramatically changes during the August Bank Holiday, when a lovely open meadow by the side of the Thames becomes the battlefield for an army of rockers. I wonder how many boats have been bottled, mooned at and even hijacked for simply passing this now not-very-tranquil spot. Nic even woke up one morning to find a dead body floating in the river.

Entering the festival site was probably the closest thing I had ever experienced to being in a cattle ranch. Upon leaving the main road we were marshalled into an arrival zone by large security people. Metal railings funnelled us towards a steward. The site was surrounded by a huge metal fence. I've since learnt that stewards at some events smile. Here, on my first trip, they looked at us grudgingly while checking the ticket and swapping it for a wristband. Nowadays, though, you're searched more intensively than boarding an EasyJet flight. Back then it was more of a glance and a question.

'Got any bottles, mate?' rattled off a rather large security guard, who was obviously sponsored by the local tattoo parlour.

'Er… no,' I replied sheepishly. I decided a smile was not worth the wrinkle.

A nod suggested clearance to enter. Words weren't the security team's main asset. I recall walking past the gate and entering the stage arena. It was in the inner sanctum, the place where at some point later on the great unwashed would hang out. I had no idea who was playing or when. David and I had a wander around, trying to look as if we hadn't just got out of the best bath ever. We probably shouldn't have, but we decided we should head to the bar. I tasted my first pint of festival ale. I must say that, even at this tender age, I had tasted better. I quickly came to the conclusion that such beers must have been brewed only to be drunk in volume or thrown across the front of the stage area. It wasn't the best ale, and certainly nothing CAMRA would vote for. That wasn't the point though. We were in and free to experience my first festival. It was time to soak everything up. Tygers of Pang Tang were on stage when we arrived – or so we found out without looking too stupid and innocent. I didn't like them.

Next up were a band called Budgie. A true rock band, but again they didn't really do anything for me. I liked the name because it reminded me of a 1960s/1970s cop programme starring the chap I was apparently named after, the cool but hard Adam Faith. Maybe some rockers reading this will be appalled by my lack of support for these bands. Taste is a personal thing. It just happens that I had grown up listening, late into the night, to the complicated structure of rock bands such as Led Zeppelin, Genesis and Pink Floyd.

I can't recall who followed Budgie. The histories say it was Gary Moore's G Force but I really can't confirm or deny this – maybe it was the effects of the beer. I'm sure, though, that if he had I would have pricked up my ears and given him due support. Def Leppard were on before the headliners Whitesnake. Weird as it seems now, David and I left before the end. This was a sampler and taster of live music at a festival in the mud; for many years to follow, it would become part of my annual itinerary. What I didn't know was that the wonderful John Peel was the DJ during some part of the event. Although my memory cells can't recall hearing him, I expect that somewhere deep down in my distant synapses I clocked his distinctive tones.

I returned to Reading Rock the following year. Even though I had only been once, I claimed it was now part of the gig-goer's year; of course at 17½ I was an expert. But it was a great time to be with friends and get slammed while listening to the 40-minute sets of anyone and everyone. Reading was the perfect venue. The Sunday set for 1981 had been watered down from the previous rock-only line-up. The promoters thought it was now ok to open up the event again to a broader range of music. The Thompson Twins were meant to play but were ill. I remember us all watching some outfit called the Desperadoes and everyone laughing their socks off at the pathetic jokes involving puns on their name.

Then I experienced something that would live with me forever. I was rapidly expanding my musical interests; at a festival I was getting a rare chance to see bands I'd never heard of.

The Enid were an eccentric Suffolk outfit, led by Robert John Godfrey. He played a wonderful French horn. It was huge; you couldn't really see him as he was lost in a sea of brass. The crowd were cool and relaxed but a bit restless by mid-afternoon. On Robert strolled with the band.

'Good afternoon Reading,' he beamed to the hippy and rocker collective in his finest public school accent. You could sense immediately that a rather stuck-up upper class bloke didn't quite fit in to this rock place. His pristine suede suit versus mud-covered Levi's. As The Enid started their set most people simply sat it out, but amazingly, as we progressed through further tracks, a few muddy rockers started to rise and then started to sway to the Genesis-like impeccably structured orchestral songs. By the end of their short set the whole crowd were on their feet, and soon the screaming hippies were demanding more. I was fascinated by the power a band could have on such a large and confrontational crowd. The Enid became legends. I later heard that their albums were major rarities.

As I crashed through my teens, Reading Rock became a *must* visit. Probably the most memorable was 1983 when a whole gang of friends decided to take in another Sunday festival event. We weren't fully fledged festival-goers but we were getting close. The highlight was seeing Thin Lizzy, fronted by the brilliant Phil Lynott.

Having already been to Reading Rock, I was now the expert. I knew how to smuggle in booze, knew where the bogs were, which bar was quickest to get served at and where best to stand.

Standing it was. No reserved seats and, at this time, no gold area for VIPs or those with fat wallets who want to be 'close to the front' without being squashed. Many of us dislike these VIP areas. For a real gig-goer these sectioned-off areas are simply ways to raise more cash, and clearly invented to cater for those who like the idea of paying extra not to be near the true hardcore fans – folk that had been there for three days and not once even thought of a wet wipe.

On this warm Sunday afternoon we gathered near the front of the stage, just a bit to the right. It was a good spot. After a few early bands came the wonderful and now almost resident The Enid, who excited the audience with their orchestral rock charms and then went. Now, the slight issue with festivals with only one stage is that the roadies have to get one band's gear off stage and then set up the next one. This takes time. No one had invented the revolving stage until Live Aid.

So in between bands the crowd had to be entertained. This was usually by a rather dodgy local DJ who would try and keep the tempo high by playing relevant tracks of the day. Of course 'dodgy DJ' does not include the late and honourable John Peel. On the other hand Reading was Reading. It was here, I'm sure, that the plastic bottle fight was invented. And it was down the front that the battle took a serious side.

Things were great this fine day, except the crowd were quite hyper, probably in expectation of the headliners Thin Lizzy. The bottle throwing was quite lively, and soon anything and everything was in the sky, raining down on anyone and everyone. The bottle battles took as long as the roadies took to change the stage. This Sunday was no different. Steel Pulse got a bad reaction from this heavy crowd. Shame, as they're such a great band.

There was a large gang of us at the festival. A few had joined in the bottle battle while the rest tried in vain to take cover. It was at this point that my mate Bob and his pal decided to throw a rather large piece of weaponry into the air. It landed with a thud.

As it hit there was one of those amazing slow-motion moments when everything went really quiet and slow. Very slow. Suddenly I noticed everyone was staring at me.

'Why? What are you looking at me for?' I thought. Then as the film slowed even further to a virtual standstill, I felt something wet and cold running down my neck. Someone let out a slight scream… but everyone else just continued to stare.

It took ages for the thump to register. The cold wet stuff seemed to be gaining in volume. I lifted my hand to my head and touched it. I drew my hand down from my damp head and looked at my fingers. It was blood. At first it didn't register. Then as slowly as the film was rolling I realised that it was blood. *My* effing blood!

Bob and his mate had now stopped laughing and were showing signs of shock. They had just thrown a large sharp pole, which originally had some Crass flag on it, some twenty feet into the air and it had landed smack bang on my bonce.

I let go a muffled 'Ow!' Clinton grabbed me.

'You ok?' he asked.

'I'm not sure.'

'Best get you to the medics,' he said, and led me off. As we were down the front the crowd was tightly crushed together. Clint grabbed my arm and pulled me through the melée. The audience parted in front of us. No one said a word. They just stared. A few yards away I turned back and shouted, 'you fucking twat, Bob!'

The medical tent was in the backstage area behind the main stage. Clint rushed me in and explained the situation very clearly. I was then examined. The nurse was straight out of *Carry on Doctor*, not so much the size but the character of Hattie Jacques. Hattie knew the answer. It involved a needle and some thread. Now, most sensible people would be extremely grateful for this free on-site service. But I was, by now, a bit hacked off, full of beer and stupidly cocky.

I turned to Hattie and said, 'sorry, but can you hurry up? Thin Lizzy will be on in a minute.'

Hattie was now well positioned above my head, her large motherly breasts at eye level with a very sharp needle in her hand. At this point the needle sped towards my wound at an increased velocity and seemed to go slightly deeper and more at an angle into my thick head than needed. Looking back, I think I got away with it very lightly. I would have stabbed anyone who spoke to me in that way. What a prat I was.

Anyway, head now sewn up, I said 'thank you' and walked back to the edge of the stage area. Clint stopped me from going back into the throng and we stood a bit further back just in time to see Phil and crew appear on stage amongst bright lights on this now cold night.

Thin Lizzy delivered an awesome set. It was full of brilliant guitars, screaming solos, drum rolls and fabulous vocals mixed with a blazing light show. The Reading crowd by now were pretty tired but Thin Lizzy had everyone jumping and cheering. We knew all the words and the event became one raucous sing-a-long.

The highlights had to be Phil's wonderful Irish lilt, supported by Gary Moore's haunting guitar riffs. I remember Phil teasing the crowd with his sexist joke: 'Are there any girls out there with a bit of Irish in them? Are there any girls who'd like a bit more Irish in them?'

He got away with it mostly because such comments were and are part of the rock 'n' roll culture. But more probably it's because it's virtually impossible to climb across the security barrier and scramble up the stage rigging without some very tattooed Hells

Angel with bulging steroid-fed muscles simply picking you up and throwing you head first back into the crowd. You would have needed more than Hattie's blunt needle to fix that.

My head hurt for a few days afterwards. I put it down to the blunt needle. Looking back I'm thankful for Hattie, whoever you were. You did a great job and I was able to see Thin Lizzy perform their last-ever live show together, ending with "Still in Love with You" – which neatly summed up my love life at this vulnerable time.

Being part of the Cambridge crew, the world-famous Cambridge Folk Festival at Cherry Hinton became a feature of the annual calendar through the 1990s. All my kids started their gigging experiences there. The beauty of the Folk Festival was that it was easy to get to, neatly set out and very compact. Perfect for buggies, young kids and chatty mums. The large grassed area outside Stage 1 was a sea of families having a summer picnic, laughing and gossiping while a variety of world folk artists strummed and fiddled away in the background. There's also a bar, which prides itself on selling more pints than the year before, exclusively dedicated to Guinness.

I managed on a few occasions to secure very elusive guest passes thanks both to BJ's lighting contacts and my real muso cousin Marc. Marc is a few years older than I and, being on my mum's side of the family line, is heavily into art and music. I'll never forget visiting his pad down at Sandbanks where he shared a basement with his mum's rather unfashionable fashion studio. It wasn't very swish but it was a place where Marc could play his music. He had his own drum kit and nervously allowed me, aged 14, to have a go.

I was so excited. This visit probably planted the drumming idea in my head. Our trip was in fact to celebrate his 16th birthday. In my mum's traditional way he was given some money to buy whatever he wanted. Fair cop to him. Rather than rush off to buy the new Hornby locomotive or Rush album, he went out and bought a brilliant silver glitter suit with four-inch-soled glitter boots… if only I had a photo.

Marc has lived the real music career throughout his life. We were never very close in our early years. I expect we were both developing our huge independent streak. We did, though, retain some very irregular form of contact. While I had ploughed – or more like gigged – through my late teens and early twenties, Marc had done the real rock 'n' roll thing. He had learnt how to light and sound a show and basically become a self-styled engineer. He could also play guitar.

I was delighted to hear that he was working at the Folk Festival in 1994. We excitedly accepted his wedding present to Jenny and me of two guest passes. Following quite a few years of no direct contact, I remember embracing him at the sound desk for Stage 2 on what was an important bonding moment.

Eric Bibb was on stage as we talked quietly and listened to a wonderful set of blues and stunning acoustic guitar. Marc, though, is a rocker. I was slightly jealous that he was of that perfect age to have been both old enough *and allowed* to see some of the best rock acts ever. His rock instincts are hard to overcome, however, and so is his preference for sheer rock volume.

So there we were chatting away, behind the sound desk, Guinness in hand, when we got a firm tap on the shoulder.

'Hey you! What do you think this is? Turn the bloody thing down,' shouted a rather small bearded man with the largest tummy ever, in a country jacket and patterned shirt. 'This is a folk festival, not a rock concert.'

Having had his say, he waddled back to the beer tent, carrying both his self-importance and empty personalised beer tankard.

Marc and I turned to each other, speechless. A few seconds passed as we let his statement filter in. We looked at the mixing desk, looked away and carried on. We did nothing. A few years later we reminisced about the event and agreed that what we should have done was to have turned the volume up and put a finger in the air. Rock 'n' roll, man!

While Cambridge Folk Festival was a good grounding for the new musos in our family, I thought they deserved something a bit more contemporary. But nothing really appealed and, importantly, nothing was reasonably local *and* affordable, except for the emerging Latitude Festival held at Henham Hall near the beautiful town of Southwold in Adnams beer country.

The Latitude event has steadily built a reputation as a family-friendly festival – partly it's the woodland setting but also they put on an eclectic range of entertainment. It's one of those rare events where you can hear quality opera followed by top comedy and then some excellent indie music. As Southwold is reasonably accessible for us, we agreed… let's go.

The 2009 event also had the added attraction of Doves and Thom Yorke playing a solo set. I've always loved Doves as they offer the classic format of a four-piece indie rock band who play powerful and edgy guitar songs. Typical of a number of indie bands, Doves were returning to the live stage after a few years away. They didn't let us down. Their set of greatest hits made me drift back to those early years when I discovered this exciting band. And their "Here it Comes" track had a beautiful video of northern soul from Wigan Hall. Amazing. I was happy, very happy.

Thom Yorke is a genius. Maybe I like him because he reminds me of my cousin Marc. Anyway, Thom has not only driven Radiohead to world fame, as I predicted, but also as a solo artist keeps his hardcore following.

The Latitude 2009 festival was sold to me on the basis of Thom Yorke's midday Sunday gig. For me this was going to be worth sharing a tent with my oldest son – something I wouldn't usually think about for a nanosecond. Thom duly performed a brilliant virtuoso musical masterclass. His short set focussed more on his newer, solo material from his acclaimed album *The Eraser*. Besides his magical journey through piano and complex guitar, we were also treated to a sampling class that involved recording some funky baselines and then looping them as a backing track while playing/singing over the top. Amazingly, Thom can get away with simply ignoring any popular classic or fan favourite. While the midday crowd screamed for those wonder hits, Thom concentrated on his set list. His own set list and no one else's. This is risky. While you can respect his musical genius, it does leave you plodding away slightly let down and – as Sunday was marred by an easterly chill and some heavy downpours – even more damp.

The good news is that the weather forced Ben and me into the large blue circus tent that housed the second stage at Latitude. I love these tents. They're real tents. Nothing like the two-man piece of material we had just spent last night in. There's something appealing about them. While they're a huge piece of canvas, lifted miles into the sky, they feel warm and cosy. At Glastonbury they're the homes of the dance sets – I suppose that's why I connect them with such good times. But for now the large blue tent offered shelter from one of those lashing storms that too often dampens (literally) a UK festival. On stage we were treated to a brilliant show from a band unknown to me: Red Light Company. It was great to hear them play a solid, lively set. Ben even took to shuffling his now cold and soaking wet feet. We hadn't come very well prepared for this downpour.

Latitude Festival takes place one week before the start of the summer holidays. Great news for kids finishing exams or preparing to leave college but not so good if you've got one more week back at school. Ben did. So as the conscientious parent and not wanting to face the scrutiny panel for poor attendance, I decided we would leave in good time, which is a painful thing for me. I hate leaving shows and events early. With bags and tent packed, we ambled over to the bus pick-up area. Jenny had taken Phibs and Sam back in the car the night before, so Ben and I were left to the mercies of public transport. While we were stuck right out on the Suffolk coast, I trusted Latitude's claim to be one of the greenest festivals. I was also comforted that Thom Yorke was there – he has calculated his own carbon footprint and won't now associate with any producer or event organiser who can't live up to their claim to be green.

We arrived at the appointed bus transfer spot. The idea was we'd get a bus to a train station, travel to Ipswich and then home to Cambridge. Ok, it wouldn't be quick, especially on engineering Sunday, but it was still do-able. The problem was that the bus depot area was empty. Completely void of any vehicle. No buses and, more worryingly, no people. This was strange as all the stewards inside the festival site and at the well-placed information points told us, and a number of other early leavers, that the buses would be every twenty minutes. This rather clear message had neither reached those outside nor, more importantly, the bus company. When someone did appear they said the buses were running every two hours. Yours truly: 'What? Every two hours? You must be joking!'

By now a few other festival leavers had arrived and were equally shocked. As the information slowly sank in, and the steward repeated the two hour message for the thirtieth time, a remarkable thing happened: a bus arrived.

Of course the arrival of a bus doesn't mean there'll be a departure. In fact, the driver was adamant he was going nowhere, as he was close to exceeding his tachograph time limit. By now the crowd was getting bigger and slightly less minded to negotiate. In fact they had more of an 'I want to go home *NOW*' mentality.

Remarkably, the will, persistence and probably the size of the crowd – coupled with all our stories of being given false information – seemed to make a genuine impression on our health-and-safety-conscious driver. He went off, coming back a few minutes later and saying: 'Ok. I'll do one trip to Halesworth station, where you can get a train to Ipswich.' A small cheer went up.

I grabbed Ben, threw our bags in the luggage hold and we jumped on. Soon a united group of gig-goers started their journey home.

Halesworth is a quaint Suffolk market town that offers a typical range of rural services and shops to the country folk for miles around – on a weekday. But this was a Sunday, so not a lot – if anything – was open, especially not around the station. The bus unloaded and we all besieged the small station platform.

I checked out the train times and then discovered we simply had no chance of reaching Cambridge today by train. Even though it was only six o'clock. I looked at a tired Ben and broke the news.

'What are we going to do?' he asked.

'Only one real option.'

'What?'

'Call your mum.' We did. Luckily mobile phones had by now taken over the world. Everyone seemed to have one. For once I approved of our technological advances.

Fortune had it that the SOS went down ok, and all we had to do was to stay put and wait. The only entertainment was reading the train times again and again, and then backwards.

Our other festival mates, though, had no other options, and were shortly joined by another busload. The Ipswich-bound platform was packed. It probably had more passengers on it than the whole station had seen all month.

A small train pulled in. It seemed nearly empty. The exception was a group of older day-trippers who were sitting, gazing happily out of the window. The train slowed to a stop. Doris, Derek, Gladys and George, I reckon, had had a lovely day out, probably by the sea, and were looking forward to a nice cup of tea.

Their happy gaze turned to shock and horror. Their mouths

opened like fish catching flies, and their eyes popped out on elastic stalks as a smelly, tired backpacked horde descended on every inch of space available. Their quiet rural train journey had just been transformed into something more akin to the Piccadilly line on a match day.

Ben and I smiled and waved as the train pulled out. Ben said, 'I'm glad mum is coming.' I grinned back, thinking, 'dead right'. So much for it being the 'greenest festival' ever. Ben and I managed to get home safely and so much quicker than on public transport. I felt let down. I was set on doing the trip environmentally but had been seriously dumped. I wrote to the organisers, Festival Republic, but in their typical fashion I didn't get a reply. Shame.

I had a much more pleasurable experience at the 2012 Latitude event, primarily as I went with my old housemate Rob and – disregarding more appalling weather – we stayed for the whole event. I fell in love with most of the festival activities, especially the I-Arena, which played home to a number of brilliant acts such as Django Django, Howler and the sheepskin hoody Zola Jesus.

The after-show entertainment was fun. We dived into the comedy tent, which had Mark Lamarr doing an excellent funky/rocky set. It was obviously so good he wanted to be a part of it, and would regularly jump into the crowd with a beer in hand and stand and listen. As I watched Mark, I noticed a business pal and greeted him like a long-lost friend. His sons were exchanging banter with him. I enjoyed seeing them all having fun somewhere out of the ordinary. I smiled. I thought how great it was to be able to go to events with your grown-up kids and enjoy great sounds and have a real laugh. I long for that day.

There was plenty to experience at the Waitrose of festivals, aka (as some call it) the new mini-Glastonbury. I felt more relaxed this time mainly as I didn't trust the transport options, and so we drove. We did share lifts, though, to protect my sustainability credentials. We'll probably come back.

I wish I could claim that my professional interest in promoting sustainability and helping us all go 'green' had some influence over festivals. Thom Yorke understood – I had hoped others would follow his example and not give us hypocritical 'greenwash.' The Isle of Wight Festival, over recent years, has also staked a claim on being green. When Nic and I went in 2007 it certainly wasn't.

The 2007 IOW festival was the first full festival Nic and I had been to together for years, and we were well up for it. It was made even better as my friend and previous charity colleague Suzanne had sold up the London high life and moved on to the island. So we decided to take her up on the offer of accommodation for the festival. It was simply too good an offer to turn down. Tent versus comfy bed? Fresh bacon butty and real coffee versus another burnt takeaway? Sorry, but we didn't even vote.

We decided to travel sustainably, and took our bikes. Once on the ferry we settled down and started the typical on-tour banter. It was great to be getting away with Nic, and we were excited seeing what the IOW Festival was about.

Nic and I are longstanding musos from very different backgrounds but bonded together by our love of great music. While we enjoy loads of similar bands, especially New Wave/punk, we also have interests at very different ends of the musical food chain. Nic loves his heavy stuff: Black Sabbath, Metallica, Slayer and more – he's got into hard trance. I respect this deeply though I leave him to it. But it's the love of music and the passion for seeing things played live that has cemented our relationship.

Of course the Isle of Wight was the place where the man himself – one of those I never saw, the one who turned a wooden instrument with six metal strings into a sex toy – had caused a riot… I'm talking about Jimi Hendrix. Admittedly this was decades earlier, but we were going there.

The main headliners on Saturday night were Muse, so there was an extra incentive for going. The Stones, playing on Sunday evening, would be interesting if only because their UK tour was sold out and pretty much cost half the IOW ticket each night.

We arrived at Suzanne's lovely house a few miles from Newport and were warmly received with tea and a choice of beers. A hot shower went down a treat. There was a good vibe, and immediately we were exchanging old stories and reminiscing over bands seen or missed.

For some reason, everyone wanted to get in to the festival on Friday night. It must have taken us well over two hours to actually get in, so we missed Echo and the Bunnymen and part of The Feeling. While we found a good space to the side of the main stage we were away from the main bar, so it was a pretty sober evening.

Groove Armada played a funky rhythm-fuelled dance set. Snow Patrol did themselves proud but were a bit too tame and laid-back for us. Nic and I wanted some noise and edge. When the bands had finished, within a few minutes of leaving the venue we were, remarkably, in Suzanne's kitchen catching up on the beers we had missed out on. The lure of a comfy bed, with a yummy breakfast the next morning, made us smile.

The Saturday line-up was the main attraction. Muse are phenomenal live. They have everything you'd want from a rock band. A huge sound, screeching guitars, blasting drums, screaming vocals, and a light and stage show of towering proportions. A few tracks into their set Nic and I looked at each and grinned from ear to ear. Wicked. We were close enough not to need words to communicate. We knew exactly what we were both feeling.

We stood at the end of a set that saw the crowd clap in unison to "Starlight," jump to the sky with "New Born" and scream to the anthem "Knights of Cydonia." Exhausted, we turned to each other and held out arms for one of those strong man bonding hugs. We had just witnessed a Top Ten set and our minds needed to be reassembled. As experienced festival-goers Nic and I then took a deep breath and took off to tour the site, looking for the after-party tent.

Earlier in the day we set out to soak up the vibe away from the stages. What I've discovered over the decades is that each festival needs its own unique appeal. Modern festivals can't get away with simply a couple of stages. There has to be raft of other stuff, such as food areas, kids' fields, a circus and a fairground. This is great for some but never really appeals to me. I get headaches even on a waltzer. Earlier in the day we mooched around and found a great show tent offering lots of local food and drink. Plenty of garlic, local sausages and pies. We stacked up our food and sought out a bench.

As we sat down to munch on our homemade sausage baguette we were approached by a couple of young smiling volunteers seeking support for their environmental charity. All would have been fine – Nic and I both strongly support ecological causes. They were asking people to sign their petition. The major problem was that the young volunteer said (and I quote): 'Our charity and the festival are keen to support the campaign *for* climate change.' I didn't need to look at Nic. His eyes just rolled and immediately his hands were clutching at his head.

It was as if a speech bubble had popped out into the air, saying *'Why did you say that? Why couldn't you have lied and said you were supporting guide dogs for destitute children in Bali. But not this...'*

Maybe they were making a weird and bad taste joke, but it was too late. My mouth had opened. The words were starting to come out. The brain was engaged. You want to discuss climate change? I was very polite, I took a few seconds, gathered my thoughts and then started. I pointed out that while every intention was to limit the event's impact on the environment much of the detail hadn't been thought through. I started to roll out my observations... the waste recycling was neither separated nor signposted properly. The bar gave out non-recyclable plastic beer containers and the beer was standard commercial piss – where was the lovely locally brewed cask ale and cider? My lecture was only a few minutes long. It was clear and accurate. But for the poor young sod it must have felt like it lasted the same length of time mankind has inflicted serious environmental damage on our earth. I vowed to complain to the organisers, which I did, when back on the mainland. I went direct to the main man as Suzanne knew him well. Surprise, surprise! I didn't hear anything back, but at least I had tried to do something.

So after Muse on the Saturday night, we went hunting for the typical small dance area or tent, which we duly found. We spent a few hours with our arms in the air bopping around to Tall Paul until late in the morning. We were surrounded by many people much younger than ourselves, but who cares? For us a festival is about the music, and we were here to find and enjoy it. We cycled home along the bike path to Suzanne's home, fully content with our musical download.

I'm informed the festival has got its act together and was awarded the Greener Festival Award in 2008. Well done.

We thoroughly enjoyed our first IOW experience, although Keith Richard's rather random solo midway through The Rolling Stones' set on Sunday was very boring.

'Thank God I didn't spend those 75 notes to see them play live,'

I shouted across to Nic. He smiled in agreement.

Apart from this I would happily return, depending of course on finances and the line-up.

Probably the most unglamorous venue I've been to was the Phoenix Festival, which was held on an old airfield at Long Marston near lovely Stratford-upon-Avon. I sensed the locals weren't too keen on this disused piece of land being invaded by loads of musos in search of a weekend of music, beer and whatever takes their fancy. It was set up in 1993 as an alternative to the other well-established events around at the time. It was also the only one held over four days rather than the traditional three.

I made two trips… not for the full weekend. My first, in 1994, was an evening trip with Ed. We sneaked out of our annual conference up the road at the University of Warwick. We preferred the sounds of The Wonder Stuff and Spiritualised to the end-of-conference disco.

A couple of years later (Thursday 18 and Friday 19 July 1996) Nic and I decided to make the trip to the Bard's county. It was made even better because we had very kindly been given some VIP backstage passes. The Thursday kicked off with a brilliant and typically powerful set from The Prodigy. They were followed by the legendary David Bowie, who headlined on the main stage. But this clashed with a rare appearance, on the Mean Fiddler Stage, by Cocteau Twins. It was a huge dilemma for me, which I'm sure everyone suffers at every festival. It feels like a conspiracy. Three hours of mediocrity then your favourite two bands at the same time, but on different stages. I decided to split my time between the two, but things didn't work out well – Liz and Robin weren't happy with the soundcheck, and it took ages before they came on stage. I noticed one of the Oxford Poly roadies running between banks of monitors and speakers trying to sort it all out. I felt for him. Meanwhile Bowie was blasting out his hits – I managed to catch a great finale, which included my favourite "Heroes." Liz, Simon and Robin swirled us with their classics but, to be honest, they were struggling with the sound, and the drum machine and backing tapes had to be reset a few times. I forgave them – others probably wouldn't – as they are one of the best bands in the world. We learnt later that the festival was in trouble. Many people hadn't got into the site in time on Thursday to see even the headliners, and water shortages during a rare hot summer didn't give the right headlines.

The Friday was wonderful, though. Perfect weather. In fact it was boiling hot. Some celebs played five-a-side footy, which was hilarious. Backstage we could lounge around, celeb spotting. I waved at Bob Mortimer. The music was fine. Alanis Morissette produced a stormer but it was the Foo Fighters who blew us all away. As I had never seen Nirvana I was excited to see how Grohl and Co. would deliver – and he certainly did, ripping through a tremendously powerful guitar rock set.

The Phoenix didn't survive. Various issues conspired against it. I enjoyed my couple of visits, but while the bands were good, the place was harsh and hard. The fences were metal and high, creating a prison feel. There was not enough grass or multi-coloured cloth to cover the yards of grey concrete. In the VIP area we were spoilt with some grass to crash out on.

Festivals have to create a vibe but the Phoenix didn't.

There's only one festival that offers so much more, while still remaining completely unique; it has a feel and ambiance all of its very own. This festival started in 1970 when punters paid £1.00 and got free milk. I wasn't allowed to go that year. Well, to be fair to my protective and supportive parents, I was only seven and had hardly taken to football, let alone going to gigs. Of course I'm referring to the one and only Glastonbury.

I first went in June 1986. I was a student and lived for live music. I probably spent more time at gigs than learning about planning policy. A number of our Oxford Poly clan decided we had earned a weekend in Somerset to listen to various bands as our reward for turning up to the odd lecture and seminar. Getting tickets for Glastonbury in 1986 was completely different from the madness of getting them these days. Back then you applied by post; today you find gangs of musos opening every laptop in the street and putting every phone on redial – and then once the booking website has opened there's the panic that you might lose your place in the automated queue.

Nic and I were well up for it. One warm Thursday morning we set off in ERD to the famous Pilton village, south of Bath. We arrived in good time. Tents, food and plenty of stuff packed. Immediately we arrived we felt a vibe, not necessarily from music –

suddenly we went quiet. There was something special in the air. It was hard to describe it. A feeling of welcome, caring, togetherness. Now, I was a late-teen muso who had seen a few things. But there was nothing that could have prepared me for the weekend ahead.

Back then it was so different from today. Firstly it was smaller. So much smaller. We found a camping field a few yards from the main stage. This field is now where they have the Other Stage. We had plenty of space to create our own camping area. Magically, there was a bloke in a VW campervan selling fudge. Lovely, homemade fudge. Yum yum. Now, I loved fudge. This was before I discovered my lactose intolerance. This smiling bloke, with unwashed curly hair, greeted me as a long-lost mate and then implied, without saying so, that his fudge was a bit different. Of course it was. Throughout all the little brown squidgy cubes were small pieces of weed. It tasted good. Damn good, man.

Drugs were part of the Glasto scene then, in the beginning, and still are today. What amazed my impressionable eyes was the openness of the trading. On the hill opposite the main Pyramid Stage was a large camping area. It offered a perfect view of the stage and festival spread out below. Through the tents was a path, which was like a town high street. Plenty of shops, but the only things on offer here were drugs. Anything and everything. Outside the various tents were small chalkboards proudly displaying the various produce… hash, coke, smack, and so on. For a Glasto virgin this was more than amazing; it was mind blowing. In some way it was a bit frightening but at the same time really liberating. Like a tourist, I just walked past thanking everyone for their kind offers. I didn't purchase.

The 1986 festival had a band list to reflect the times. We had Level 42, Madness, Psychedelic Furs, Simply Red and The Housemartins. All of whom played great sets. But the pull for me was the chance to see my favourite band, The Cure. The Cure had never headlined Glasto and were billed for Saturday night. While for most of the weekend it was warm and dry, as the evening set in the clouds gathered, and by mid-evening it had started to rain.

Nic and I settled in a good spot near the front of the main stage. Lloyd Cole and the Commotions had played a great set and the roadies were working hard to put up The Cure's kit and simple set. Precisely at 10:15 pm, The Cure appeared on stage and charged straight into "10.15 on a Saturday Night." Perfect timing. We went mental, jumping around shouting and screaming.

I was by then a bit drunk and full of fudge. Looking around I noticed a small group who were still chatting and sitting on the grass. As a way of looking after my favourite band I started to give them some slight abuse. Nic was trying to calm me down but not doing very well.

'It's The Cure, Nic. All these people can do is chat and sit on their arses.'

Luckily The Cure were giving out a reasonable noise. Suddenly the group realised the band were on stage and stood up and started to join in the fun. I mockingly applauded them. It was then that one of them turned round. To my shock and surprise, I knew this person. It was Jenny, my friend from Oxford. The person I would eventually fall in love with and, a few years later, marry.

'What you doing here?' I said stupidly.

'Coming to Glastonbury,' she replied innocently to my pathetic question.

'Ha ha, very funny,' I mocked. She didn't smile, so I apologised.

We then spent a few tracks catching up, probably pissing everyone else off around us. At the end of the set we said goodnight. No Glasto romance – we left that to a few years later when we got married.

'You do get an odd mix at these festivals,' I said to Nic as we trudged back to our tents.

The 1986 Glasto was also badly timed. Not on Michael Eavis's part; he always chose the weekend around or after the summer solstice. The 1986 Glasto was the same weekend that FIFA had decided to play the quarter-finals of the World Cup. On Sunday, 22 June 1986, late afternoon, England had been drawn to play Argentina. Thatcher had tried to derail things a few years before by engaging in a war to save the Falkland Islands. Now it was our footy teams who were doing battle. But here we were in a muddy field in Somerset getting high, drunk and lost in music without any forms of modern technology or communication media. Except one.

I never knew why or even asked but some bloke had brought along a good old battery-driven radio. He was in a tent only a few yards from the main stage and – in true festival sharing mode – he brought it outside for everyone to listen to the commentary.

About a hundred footy fans gathered around his tent listening to the equivalent of Five Live and Bryon Butler's soon-to-be-famous commentary. Simply Red followed by Madness were on the Pyramid stage but we were focussed on the game. All of us footy blokes could only picture the scene as Maradona scored his 'Hand of God' goal. England lost. I remember walking away sad and disappointed. Luckily Madness were still on stage – in an instant I was back at the festival. Music saved the day, but only just. Level 42 were on immediately afterwards. We watched them quietly and then left for home before the evening headline act, who was Gil Scott-Heron. We had enjoyed a great weekend. Our survival strengthened my desire to return.

Glastonbury has been a regular event on my gig scene calendar ever since. It's a non-negotiable annual homage. I still love the excitement of preparing to head down to Somerset for the best festival in the world. Yes, it has changed considerably over the years, though some of its key elements are still in place. The variety of entertainment continues but the line-ups have arguably become more commercial and less relevant to many of the guests. But for me and my close mates it remains amazingly eclectic, wonderfully natural and perfectly varied. At the same time it offers so much more than any other festival. It's simply a festival on a different level.

Popularity has forced through some major changes. 1500 enjoyed their first festival in 1970; 175,000-odd battled through an internet nightmare then had to face a real mud bath in 2011. Twice a year it manages to crash the whole internet system across the land: every muso laptop and computer is standing by to receive that all-important booking form – once completed, it means you've secured your ticket. My friend Keith organises us with military precision. Paul and Leslie staff the work computers for extra bandwidth and internet speed. No one is allowed anywhere near the router just in case we *do* get through. It's painful, bloody painful. I feel my heart race when the message that the system is blocked disappears, closely followed – I'm hoping – by the booking page…

I've been cynical about the process over the past few years. Michael, why not hold a ballot or, even better, reward those regulars with a first-chance booking service? Anyway, whichever way, I'll be there. Some, though take drastic measures. This year

(2013) Ken, besides coming over from Perth - in Australia - is having to get the coach from Edinburgh; to make matters worse Stu, who lives only an hour away from the site, is going with him. I can't stop crying it's so funny. Me? I'm going from Bath.

For a few decades now this part of beautiful Somerset has become a walled city. Literally. The hills and vales of this rural idyll are, over a few days, dominated by a massive metal fence 12 feet high. Security is now so heavy it must be easier to get into Baghdad. In the 1990s and especially 2000, thousands of gatecrashers simply climbed over the fence. Each had their own plan. Some dug tunnels, others brought ladders. In 2000 the famous wall was staffed by a load of lads from Merseyside and Manchester. The atmosphere was unpleasantly tense.

'Give us a tenner and you can climb over,' smiled some bloke from Liverpool, pointing to a metal fold-up ladder resting next to the metal wall.

'No worries, I've got a ticket,' I said.

'What did you get that for?' said the young man from that northern city on a large river, suggesting I was mad. His eyes rolled around his spaced-out head.

I didn't feel that a rational conversation or, in fact, any form of dialogue would be worth it.

It was also the year that Oasis were the Saturday headliners. The crowd were tense and there was angst in the air. Loads of lads – many of whom had crashed in and were all pissed up – created a tense, unnerving atmosphere. Many just seemed to be edgy, wanting a fight. It wasn't nice. Oasis played a loud, cocky set. It was ok but Oasis were on their mega-ego trip by this time. I watched a few opening tracks and thought 'no'. I wanted something different and headed up to Shangri-La.

In the noughties things became more controlled. Costs rose, the fence was built like the Berlin Wall, and the acts were more diverse and cross-genre. In recent years we've seen debates arise as to whether rappers like Snoop Dogg should be on the bill. I'm not fussed. It's a contemporary music and arts festival, so why not? There are hundreds of other acts to see.

While much has changed, many things haven't. There's no other festival that offers the true friendship and bonding vibe. Nowhere can you sit on a hay bale next to the cider bus and end up chatting away to some complete stranger in such an open and happy way. Long live Glasto.

Even though I can't walk home from it after an evening, Glastonbury remains *the* festival for me. So you can imagine how appalled I was to hear people, at last year's event, saying they were there just because they 'had to do a Glastonbury once' – a kind of tourist sign off. Look, Glasto is mega and cannot be patronised by those of us who have been going for years. But it's not and never should be a museum piece. While it can't be an elitist club of old hippies it must not become something to do just the once. What next, City Sightseeing Tour buses going around the perimeter?

'Oh, Tarquin – fancy going to Somerset for that *Glarstonbury* fest thing?'

'Yar, should be triff.'

'Who's playing?'

'Oh, I've no idea. We just need to go once to say we've been there. Tick it off the list. Oh yar, we can get one of those tepees, it'll be really cool. We won't need to use those smelly toilets. Do Jasmine and her lovely friends want to come?'

Shame, because the real Glasto is significantly more than a tick-box thing to do before you're 30. It mustn't become a bucket list event. Glastonbury is, admittedly, an adventure, and each year it offers something new to explore, enjoy and recount. It's also part of a muso's annual cycle of events. While for some people their year consists of Cheltenham Races, Chelsea Flower Show, Royal Ascot, Wimbledon and Lord's for the Test, for a muso our year has a trip to HMV for the sales in January, a set of local gigs in early spring, a visit to London for the up-and-coming band who released tickets last September, then in the summer a couple of festivals and possibly one big outdoor gig. Glastonbury is simply *the* annual festival. Over time it has become a pilgrimage; it now feels like some sort of homecoming.

When my kids started to show interest in music I thought it would be good to take them to a festival. But Glastonbury is reserved as *my* retreat, *my* special event. Even though they constantly ask me to go, I'm not taking them... not yet anyway. They too should start to enjoy the variety and fun of a festival, but maybe not with me.

I'm on a roll now with Glastonbury attendances. Throughout the noughties it was where Ken, Stu and I spent our annual hedonistic lads' weekend. It's an important time for us to meet up, drink beer, laugh, buy Pilton Porker burgers, laugh, jump around arm in arm, laugh and laugh even more. There's a big clan in our Glasto posse now, and I'm eternally grateful to Paul, Leslie and (sometimes) Keith for heading off days in advance to get us a good camping spot. For us, Glastonbury is the quintessence of what a festival should be about. A place where you can dress and do whatever you want. Here I've seen people naked, covered in mud, or wearing dinner suits; hippies, punks, rockers and rastas; and whole gangs decked out in full army battle garb. I've seen bowler hats, top hats, wigs of every colour, and every make of boot.

And there's so much variety. The comedy area, the cinema tent, a kids' field larger than some festivals themselves. The folk tent, the fire-eaters, the tea ladies. There's the World Stage (I camped near for a few years… 'downtown,' I called it), the Other Stage, and now The Park. Each stage is beautifully decorated by dedicated Glasto folk. And the oil drums are covered in coloured plastic where we carefully sort our waste. The beautiful flapping prayer flags.

The music line-ups are simply mind-blowing. There are literally thousands of acts. One to please everyone. I love it when meeting someone who has never been before. You can see the excitement in their eyes. It just gives everyone a buzz. As someone who has reached the 'ten club,' I feel privileged to pass on my worldly advice.

'You do realise it takes two hours to cross the site.'

'Select only a few bands you really want to see… then fill in the time exploring. You'll stumble across some act, show, band, artist, event which will make the whole trip worthwhile…'

Glastonbury is special. Very special. It's also made by all the wonderful sideshows. The Arcadia, Shangri-La, the theatre area, Avalon. We've seen every kind of band out there. We even saw the re-formed Wombles. Ken, Stu and I cried with laughter for hours having spent an hour in the Temple Dedicated to Bono puppet tent, where we did karaoke to a packed crowd while dancing the puppets of Bono and The Edge.

Besides all the music, there are places – as in any community – where you can chill out. Even in Glastonbury you can, incredibly, find an area of silence and calm. The Green Fields and Healing Fields offer the perfect places to relax, take a massage, meditate, admire the beautiful stones, drink chai or have an excellent full organic breakfast. An army of helpers keep these gems buzzing through day and night. And everyone smiles… even when it's tipping down.

Glastonbury is huge but every inch is covered in something… whether it's people, music, artists, art, stalls, smells, bottles or trodden mud, there's absolutely nothing like it. Yes, I dream back to the days when I first came along, when things were less crowded, less commercial, and more natural. But every time I go, I find a place where I can sit on a bench and meet new friends, engage in happy trivial banter, share muso stories, people-watch and laugh until the Eavis cows come home.

When things are tough, life too hectic, I dream of that perfect late afternoon when I head over to the Glade, a small stage surrounded by trees near the old railway line. Here in its own little world you can watch the sun set and listen to some classic DJ or trance band. Your feet and heart start to beat without prompting. If there's a place to be, where you can float away to a classic set of *old skool* trance from esteemed DJs like the fabulous Nick Warren or Toby Marks, the Glade is it.

Yes, the loos smell, but even their odour has a certain uniqueness. So much so that I bet if you could bottle it you'd make a fortune. Imagine having a little pot on your work desk – when things are tough you can release a bit of the odour and it'll send you back to those green metal stalls where you daren't look down, and you'll say 'I miss that.'

I've been privileged to see many of my favourite artists here and many I'd never thought of as such: Arctic Monkeys, Snoop Dogg (even if all he can do is swear), Tame Impala, Dizzee Rascal. Then there's the legendary early evening headliner on the Saturday where we've been graced with vocal legends such as Dame Shirley Bassey, Sir Paul McCartney, Sir Tom Jones and Neil Diamond. In one short weekend I can indulge in every musical taste, from heavy rock, pure indie, passionate soul, artful jazz, blissful reggae to trippy trance.

Perfect. Bloody perfect.

Seven: **Flat Champagne and Egos**

Rise up this mornin'
Smile with the rising sun
Three little birds
Pitch by my doorstep
Singin' sweet songs
Of melodies pure and true
Saying, 'This is my message to you'

"Three Little Birds" by Bob Marley and the Wailers

THE TROUBLE WITH LIKING LOTS of different bands is that you get tempted to see lots of gigs. Like the quantity versus quality debate, some simply don't – or at least didn't for me – live up to their studio recordings. Like anything in life, nothing is perfect – certainly not all the time. I'm pleased and proud to say that I've only ever been to a handful of *bad* gigs. A testimony to damn good taste, I say. Surprisingly, though, some of the worst performances have, in fact, come from bands you would probably buy a ticket on eBay to go and see.

I'm sure many of us have come out of a gig and gone, 'well, that was alright... Not their best set' or even, 'shame that *blah* happened.' It's rarer that you leave the gig saying, 'that was bloody awful,' or, even worse, leave mid-set.

I'm also pleased to say that I cannot recall ever leaving a gig, with the band still playing, because they were so bad. I'm very proud of that. I do admit, though, having to take a break during the Motorhead gig at Reading University in 1984 simply because my ears were hurting so much I thought my head was about to explode. This particular gig was blasting and is probably the main cause of damage to my hearing. It was even louder than the AC/DC gig I was lucky to see with school pal Rob when staying at his gaff in Canada one school holiday. Inside the ice hockey stadium during this gig, AC/DC actually fired off a cannon. So compete with that. Even with my ears ringing louder than Bow Bells I did re-enter to see the last few tracks and encore. But that was loud, very loud. As I'm writing this I can feel a pain in my left ear starting to get worse.

Now, this chapter may shock a few people. I'm expecting and preparing for various band members to call for a fatwa or threaten my son's hamster to make me retract the comments that follow. But amazing as some bands think they are, some simply did not live up to their ego.

There was one artist I was keen to see, and that was the Godfather of Funk: the one and only Mr James Brown. I had missed a few of his earlier visits to the UK but managed to catch up with him at Brixton Academy in June 1988. This was before the September of that year when his nastier side grabbed hold of his mind. He was given six years in prison for a gun-wielding car chase. Arguably I shouldn't have gone and paid to see this man. Brown, regarded by many as the 'hardest-working man in music,' was also an alleged wife beater. But my musical respect overrode my moral values and off I went.

It was probably another case of high expectations, but right from the start it all felt just too quick. I love funk music. I wish I could dance to it, but then again how many white guys from well-to-do backgrounds can dance properly anyway? Funk is one of those styles that grabs you around the waist and puts speed into your legs. I was up for a good dance but each track the Godfather bashed out was just too pacey. I lost interest and the plot. Most folk around me appeared to be enjoying themselves, but however hard I tried I couldn't get it. It began to feel like a tour out of desperation. The need to be somewhere else. 'Quick, let's get some gigs on, earn a bit of cash, get my name out there again and hope we don't get lynched by lots of angry women…' I left Brixton feeling my soul train had just, Ronnie Biggs-style, been robbed. Shame. I watched the news intensely a few months later when the story of his mad rage came out. He probably wasn't very well, I tried to justify to myself.

New Order's "Blue Monday" was a defining track for me. It came at a time when my life was taking off. I was on a roll. I was developing new friendships through various school connections who loved music and parties. With a good-sized record collection I'd often become the party DJ. My new friends were also enjoying life. Many of us were reaching milestone birthdays, and with them came parties… lots of them. In particular my close friend Clare and her sister Helen invited me to come to celebrate Clare's 18th birthday party. Clare and Helen were girl friends in the pure form. Although they were gorgeous my eyes were glued on Fiona. Even while misty in love, I still partied, so the invite was rapturously accepted. And of course it was a chance to be DJ. The top tune was "Blue Monday." I remember playing it virtually non-stop. We all loved it. It was something different, unique and went on for ages. I was blessed with a wonderful 12-inch version in a kind of floppy disc black cover. It even had a couple of cuts in the sleeve side. Like all my records, I still have it safely stashed away. Every time I hear it I can see us all dancing around Clare and Helen's living room full of energetic youth.

New Order, however, were renowned for being a bit stroppy. They certainly lived up to their reputation as being really moody when they came to the Oxford Apollo in the spring of 1986. I eagerly expected a great set and a chance to dance away to their various classic tracks. The evening got off well with the local Goth band Chatshow taking us on a glorious ride through their guitar epics – shame they never really made it. Anyway, I had heard about Bernard Sumner's moods but rather put it aside. New Order came on stage to a warm welcome, and soon we were bopping away to their electronic vibe. I was right down the front and leaning on the stage.

After what felt like 45 minutes or so some muppet – or plonker, as people used to say in those days – threw a bottle on to the stage. Mid-track, Bernard stopped playing. He looked at Peter and then they simply walked off stage. A few words were lipped to the crowd, but nothing else. We stood and waited. Nothing. The crowd begged them back with a slow handclap. But nothing. The crowd, getting restless, started howling and catcalling. Still nothing. After an age the house lights went on and we were told that New Order were pissed off with people throwing things on stage and that they weren't coming back. Now, that really was a bloody Blue Monday.

I bought tickets to see Lou Reed play at the lovely Brixton Academy in the early 1980s. But for some reason they never arrived. It was those days of pot luck ticket booking where you sent cheques and a neatly stamped addressed envelope. For some strange reason I didn't chase them up. So I never saw Mr Take a Walk on the Wild Side. I've never been a massive fan but Lou Reed was one of those icons on that 'must-see' list. Everyone has a bucket-list of bands to see before you meet them in the sky.

So when he announced a gig at the wonderful Junction in Cambridge in April 2010, I thought, well, this is probably the last chance to see him, and it's only down the road. This gig, however, wasn't Lou Reed doing a special greatest hits tour. It was one of his offshoot projects, called the Metal Machine Trio. Now, I support artists wishing to experiment. They're artists. Someone is bound to like it, you hope.

Metal Machine Trio was very different. How can I put it politely? Well, I suppose on first hearing it was like a listening to a hammer drill breaking up tarmac and concrete. There were additional scratching sounds rather like metal nails scraping down a rusty piece of iron. All very industrial. It was played fast and loud. This was a band with a variety of instruments, which they appeared to be playing live. But unless you're an expert, I would have no idea whether it was a *Top of the Pops*-style mime or not. There weren't many, if any, vocals to recall. It was in fact a gig of pure white noise.

I was pleased to see a large turnout for this unique affair but I expect many of my fellow gig-goers were attending out of intrigue. We wanted to see what all the hype was about. With most gigs, though, I recognise more or less most of the tracks. With this one I have to claim I knew absolutely nothing; I genuinely cannot name one single piece of noise. I expect to be enlightened, at some later date, with a copy of the track listing. It will probably contain tracks such as "Grrrrurggh," "Rrrrrrrawwwwwo" and the fabulous "Eeeekkrrrrgggghhh." After about four 'noise things' I actually thought none of them had track titles. Give Lou his due, he stuck to his script and played absolutely nothing remotely memorable or officially recognisable.

By about half way through the so-called 'set' I noticed that the small bar area was packed, no doubt full of bemused gig-goers going, 'what the fuck is *that*?' The crowd were restless and, like the tide, going out fast. I'm pleased to say I stuck it out and watched a frowning Lou leave the stage amidst probably the weakest applause ever. I left the gig thinking this is the type of event that, on one hand, shows that music can be raw, primitive and completely off the far end of the scale. On the other hand, it will feed the critics for years. Good job Thatcher and her cronies aren't around or we'd have another stupid piece of legislation requiring all music to have a vocal, some form of basic four-beat rhythm and only to be played to people dressed in dinner suits. I'll put that down to experience and cross Lou Reed off my 'musicians to see before I die' list. I had seen him now and that was enough.

One of the most famous experimentalists in the music business and other more illegal things (allegedly) is the squire himself: Mr D. R. Jones, or – as we know him – David Bowie. The Brixton-born artist of many guises, sexual intrigue, genius and that famous half-coloured eye. I've been fortunate to see Bowie on a few occasions. At least two of his shows – the Serious Moonlight Tour at Milton Keynes Bowl in 1983, and his Sunday headline act at Glastonbury in 2000 – were bloody awesome.

In 1989, though, he was tinkering with a unit called Tin Machine. Two years later (November 1991) I was delighted to hear he would be playing the Cambridge Corn Exchange. Luckily, I managed to pull off getting a ticket without queuing for days and hours. On the night, along with many of the other lucky punters with tickets, I was slightly unsure what to expect. We arrived earlier than standard, just in case he did something very weird like start with a Bowie support act of greatest hits. We waited in vain. He wasn't his own support act. A few of us had actually bought the album but I know that virtually nobody could name a track from it. There weren't any 'hits,' there was no space man, no Ziggy, no Major Tom. No anthem track and certainly no heroes. But like the curious muso I am, I was keen to see Bowie in my adopted home venue.

The show was finely tuned and Bowie was supported by a great bunch of session musicians. However… I didn't get it. The songs were ok, but nothing made the show stand out. There was nothing to make you go, 'wow, that was brilliant.' Even the light set was simple and boring. As the gig wore on, I knew the experiment wasn't working and that the Tin Machine would soon have to be recycled, hopefully into the genius we all expected. I left the venue by the side entrance just as Bowie was being hustled into a waiting black limo. I *so* wanted to ask him what he thought of the show… then again it was probably best left answered, and we all moved on.

The Tin Machine gig should have taught me a lesson. I needed to be careful about whom I saw, especially those huge icons claiming to have rediscovered themselves. It should also have warned me that not even a superstar can churn out a Top Ten gig every time. But then again, if we don't experiment, how do we learn?

I carried on seeing virtually every band in Cambridge who were either on the circuit or had something new to offer – until I saw Chris Isaak. The human hulk came from a humble background in the States, where his apparent good looks and strong blues and folk guitar attracted a bit of cult following. Chris became famous in the late 1980s for film roles, including a role in David Lynch's *Twin Peaks*, but it was his voice that set him out from the crowd. In 1989 he produced the single "Wicked Game," following up with an album and the typical promotional tour. The UK tour had been well endorsed and I decided to take a trip down to the Corn Exchange to see him. My God, I wish I hadn't. I don't think I've ever been so bored at a gig in my life. I admit that at some events, mainly due to work, late-night TV and a few beers, I've been tired and have, embarrassingly, let out the odd yawn. Not good I know.

But this set was dire, *so* dire. By track three his monotonous voice had me yawning. The crowd didn't help and were about as mobile as our veteran football team's defence. I could only hope that my fellow gig-goers were feeling the same pain and just wanted it to finish. My fear is that some poor sod went to this gig, brimming full of excitement – just like I was at my first gig – and that this muppet put him or her off for life. Luckily for me, I simply wrote it off. Isaak: large black felt-tip pen through name on the bands-to-see register. Not every gig can be the best in the world. I know that. I'm a realist but sadly some artists take us muso punters for granted. Well, sorry Chris, you didn't fool me. You're fired.

Robert Allen Zimmerman, aka Bob Dylan, has to be one of the most influential musicians ever. Maybe even *the* most. Not only has he written and produced some of music's most poignant and inspirational songs, he did one thing that arguably changed music for ever. In 1965, at the Newport Folk Festival, he picked up and plugged in an electric guitar. Famously, the next year, while playing Manchester Free Trade Hall, the now fully wired-up Dylan (and band) passed into music folklore, condemned by a member of the crowd as a Judas. Why Dylan went electric I've no idea. It might have been a well worked strategy. On the other hand he may simply have found himself without a tuned acoustic instrument. Worse still, maybe someone nicked it? But that moment created more guitar heroes than metal strings, more long hair growth and more brilliant new bands. Of course I wasn't there but I wish I had been. I was only one year old. No chance.

Now here's the difficult bit. Of course Dylan is an icon. He is a world-changer, an inspirer, a rebel and for many a reason to live. To many he is a God, to others he is the knight in shining folklore. However, live, I found him as boring as, I personally find the *Daily Mail* appalling. I expect I've now upset quite a lot of people, but stay with me.

I've seen Dylan twice. Once in 1981 at the Earls Court hangar, and then some twelve years later at the Fleadh festival in Finsbury Park, north London. I liked the Fleadh because it was raw and, in best Irish tradition, the *craic* was good. Things were made even better as I was very kindly offered guest tickets through my late triend Duncan. He managed to pull off some sponsorship whizz through his City finance pals. No need for Nicki and the A&R trick this time, even though I was an established well in-tune and highly respected DJ through the early 1990s. Well sort of.

Things reached new heights: not only did I have freebie tickets but I could also make full use of the guest area, including clean, non-toxic-smelling loos complete with dry loo roll. Plus a minor bonus: the VIP area had access to a bar without any queues. Heaven. Of course, this being the Fleadh, the beer wasn't the usual watered-down stuff you normally get, but true, pure, cold Murphy's. Admittedly I prefer Guinness but I know that important lesson: never be ungrateful for a good pint.

I couldn't quite believe it when I strolled up to the portakabin on the edge of the park and picked up the tickets from a smiling and helpful member of staff. I was then shown to a special barrier and walked in. I recall it was a warm summer's day. The crowd were excited but not hostile.

The beauty of college for me was that I had found myself a really close set of friends who fortunately stuck together for our socialising even though we were living in different parts of the country. A number of us came to the Fleadh to catch up on old times. We were all growing up and slowly becoming part of the working establishment. Our career journeys had started. Living in new places meant lots to share. It wasn't long before someone suggested a beer. Of course they all looked at me, and off I toddled off to the VIP section to the side of the stage.

While I relished having VIP tickets, it also meant I had to offer back. So with the knowledge of free booze I took it upon myself to keep the group well watered. As a novice to VIP treatment I was a bit nervous of being sussed out or being asked some unique password someone had forgotten to tell me. So I put on a confident face and walked up to the security guard. My pass checked, I was in. I was in that inner sanctum. A place I had imagined and hankered after. But sadly I was let down. There weren't champagne bottles in coolers on every bench or table, or wild naked dancers swinging from high wires. No, just normal folk, like you and me, collecting their free booze, chatting and laughing without needing to queue.

I wandered up to the bar and ordered an almost un-cartable number of pints, reached for my wallet and then was very politely informed that the drinks were on the house. Bargain! I failed in disguising my wonderful surprise. I carefully wedged the pints between my palms and headed back, undeniably at a snail's pace. My purpose was clear. I was being considerate. But I arrived to a moaning gang who could only say, 'where the fuck have you been?'

'Getting you a free pint, you tight arse,' I replied rather sharply.

The whole day was spent making this trip. Towards the end of the afternoon I had now sped up somewhat and didn't care if in the mid-afternoon sunshine on the way back I recklessly dropped half the pint on someone sleeping. The bands were a bit unnoticeable, really. Mary Black, Van 'the man and his hat' Morrison. Hot House Flowers improved things and got most of the crowd up off the grass. There was also the excellent Stiff Little Fingers. It needed some edge. Dylan, though, was probably the one act most of the punters had come to see. I was excited to see this legend, a man who has sold zillions of albums. I was intrigued that, even at this time, he had a back catalogue larger than my whole collection. I was also looking for one of those gigs that would blow your mind. I wanted it to make me join every radical campaign group on earth, stop me washing in anything but fresh rainwater and make me feel like charging off to change the world single-handed.

If only. Do you know that, to this day, I cannot recall one good song he sang or played? His stage presence suggested he was in fact dead and that a doppelganger had replaced him. Yes, it was great to see the man himself. Yes, it was great to hear his famous throaty vocal, but as for a show – well, I came away thinking it wasn't very good. Understatement of the bleedin' decade. The post-event analyses agreed, and for the first time that day we were all united in consensus.

Hard as this is to say, and I still find it unbelievable, but the band that let me down the most has to be the Happy Mondays at Cambridge Corn Exchange in 1992. The thing was this. On paper and billboard this was, and should have been, the gig that changed the world. An instant Top Ten gig. But it wasn't. In fact for various reasons it was immediately put into the bottom ten and threatened with relegation.

Sunday evening is, admittedly, never a good night for a pounding dance attack. Most folk are preparing for work or even school the next day. Sunday is the recovery day from heavy evenings on Friday and Saturday. But when it was announced that probably one of the most famous and influential bands of their time and virtual gods from Madchester were coming to our Corn Exchange there was simply no debate. I was going.

Happy Mondays stormed the music world in 1988 exactly when everyone was searching for something new. And they got it spot on. By 1992, Happy Mondays had produced two of the most iconic albums of the time, *Bummed* and *Pills 'n' Thrills and Bellyaches*. Both offered hope in those times of despair. Both offered a new formula of loud guitar supported by tribal beats and slightly out-of-tune vocals from a drug-driven Shaun Ryder.

Besides their dazzling studio sound, Happy Mondays were gaining acclaim for a strong live set where the famous Bez would dance around the stage with maracas, half crazed, half stoned. It was a brilliant idea.

So with the hype and media frenzy at boiling point, my expectations were high. Probably too high.

We were well set up for Happy Mondays. The problem was they weren't there. In fact they were not even in Cambridge or anywhere near. As the time between acts lengthened and lengthened, the crowd got more and more restless. It got to a point when we started to call for the Stereo MCs to come back on. A brave announcer informed the now impatient and knackered crowd that Shaun and posse were on their way, but not quite… out of Manchester.

'Wot? Manchester is bloody miles away. I have work in the morning.' Politely we waited and waited. It must have been nearly an hour and half by the time they eventually arrived and by this time loads of people had gone and the faithful were either pissed off or nearly asleep.

Credit to Shaun, when they did arrive they went straight into their set. Bez was jumping and charging around but his energy just drained mine. The Happy Mondays gave a good belting to "Step On" and "Kinky Afro" with great gusto but by now I was knackered and yawning far too often. It just didn't work. The Mondays' music, funky and important as it was at this time, made little impression on me. But the damage had been done. My expectations had been raised too high. I left feeling really let down and vowing not to go back.

It's a huge let-down when as a paying guest you feel that your hard-earned dosh hasn't quite taken you to seventh heaven. That the show you just witnessed hasn't opened the door to your inner soul. But this is live music and it's part of the deal. You have to take the odd missed note, the broken drumstick and the occasional poorly mixed vocal. Watching live music is like any album; there will be stand-out moments, those anthem songs mixed with the odd one where you just press skip or lift up the needle every time. It's often these let-down moments that make those nights of ecstasy (not the drug) just get better and better. I can take the odd poor show; it just makes me a bit more cautious in my older years.

Eight: **Down the Front**

Come on
Throw your hands up
If you've got the feeling
Jump across the ceiling

"Jump" by House of Pain

I HATE SITTING AT A GIG. Let's be honest, what's the point? The whole idea, I thought, about seeing music live is being able to dance and jump around. You have the freedom and space to move. It's music we're talking about, not a poetry recital. So how can you dance when your bum is firmly seated in some uncomfortable plastic seat… the type you find at various football grounds, designed for Mr and Mrs Small? They never seem to fit. It doesn't matter where you are, these cheap pieces of furniture are always bloody cold even at the height of an epic heat wave. Plush theatres are exempted but if the gig is too quiet you risk nodding off, and that's simply not on.

    Of course some people have to sit for health reasons – fair enough. I'm pleased to see that event managers have arrived in the real world over recent years and now provide good space and viewing platforms, at most events, for people with disabilities. Ok, not all are perfect and many really excellent venues have struggled hard to meet the requirements for disabled access to public buildings. I also know… but don't tell anyone… that some venues I refuse to name legitimately sell tickets for disabled people to able-bodied souls when the allocation is not taken up by the time limit. This little scam has served me well on the odd occasion over the years.

Back to the point. Why do people buy tickets to sit at a gig? Surely you know you won't be close to the stage. Those lovely front row seats only seem to end up in the hands of eBay traders. What happens too when your girlfriend gets up and starts bopping around and the bloke behind, who is seated simply due to his rather large frame, says, 'hey, love, sit down, I can't see the stage.' It makes for a potentially nasty little scene that, once started, can go totally out of control and end up with you missing the one and only track you knew and wanted to hear.

I remember being at a Level 42 gig at the massive Wembley Arena hangar when some drunken prat in the row behind pushed me repeatedly in the back for standing up. It was all very amusing to his cronies. Luckily one of the girls in his crowd saw sense and told him to piss off to the bar. I still have one of those daydreams where I follow him downstairs to the bog and, while he tries to relieve himself of his twenty pints of Carlsberg, (kind of) by accident land him a right hook that makes him fall face down in his own piss.

Yes, I admit to sitting at some gigs but this is never out of choice. Some venues only offer seats, such as those hangars of all hangars, O2 Arena or Earls Court. Of course I've also been to see bands play at various theatres where the seats can't be removed. I recall seeing the lovely laid-back and calming Everything But the Girl (Tracey Thorn and Ben Watt) play at the Bloomsbury Theatre in London. I suppose being seated was very fitting for this tranquil, melodic, wonderfully soothing evening out. It was also a Sunday evening and we were knackered from a big night clubbing in Camden. This was fine. It worked.

But again, why would you choose to sit at a gig? Unless you get your tickets early at many larger venues, the chances are you'll be sitting miles from the stage; even those huge screens will just be specks in the distance, lost in the dry ice and twirling light display. The sound is so out of sync that the band have actually left the stage before you start to applaud their last track.

I wonder what the so-called 'mega bands' think when playing huge footy stadia in front of tens of thousands of adoringly generous fans who have paid more than a day's wages to sit so far away that NASA has to send up a satellite to beam back the whole event. Do they give a damn?

I smiled broadly recently when I was at that better-than-average hangar, the National Indoor Arena in Birmingham. Guy Garvey from the sublime Elbow called out the name of some bloke who was possibly the furthest away from the stage.

'Hey. Can we shine a light on the back please?' Guy said to the lighting crew. 'Can John Bloggs (*not his real name but I'm sure he was a John*)... Can you stand up? Are you seated in Block Bloody Miles Away, Row Z Seat Infinity?' Guy says. Good job he had a mic.

After a few minutes' lag in reacting, John Bloggs obligingly waves back to Guy and all the audience way below. I bet everyone standing around me – I was at the front, of course, slightly to stage right – looked up and thought, 'why the fuck are you sitting up there? Are you mad?' Oh, I get it. The best mate was left to buy the tickets via Ticket Toutmaster and by the time he or she had been able to sneak online at work one Friday morning, the only tickets left were these, or a couple near the stage but with an obstructed view.

Mr Bloggs would have been gutted if he ever found out his tickets were no cheaper than ours. We could hear and see everything in real time. He couldn't have.

My aversion to sitting comes from the era I grew up in. I started seeing bands back in 1979 – just at the end of the mad punk era and when music was revving up big time. The music I was listening to and wanted to see live was all about jumping around.

Reading was not famed for its music venues at this time. As well as the rather steady Hexagon we also had one of those classic late 1970s venues where there were no lights and everything was black except for some red light over the bar: the Top Rank Club. The floor was permanently damp from the beer spills and the odd bit of blood from the traditional evening punch-up. Underneath was the cold and desolate bus station.

This was where all the up-and-coming bands played in Reading, especially the harder ones. We were there for raw sound – and there was lots of it. But it was the jumping around that me and my mates loved.

It was here that I discovered what we simply referred to back then as being 'down the front' – that space about four rows back from the stage where every head case and nutter would pogo as if on speed, pounding into anyone who dared enter. Here arms flailed in any direction. Indiscriminate punching of everyone – including your best buddy – was rife.

At the age of 17 and from a very nice/closeted home, being down the front was everything the *Daily Mail* and Thatcher hated. It was the zone for uncontrolled youth to be uncontrolled and anarchic. If in the late 1970s Thatcher and her cronies ever wanted to round up the riff-raff they should simply have sent the boys in blue into every Top Rank Club across the land and drag us into the blue van.

Amongst everyone baying to be down the front (or, in current parlance, 'in the mosh pit') there was a real sense of comradeship. It was irrelevant who you were and where you came from. It didn't matter which school, which road or which part of town. Down the front you were all one. We were all here to jump around, drink beer and scream loudly with our heroes on stage. Going down the front was scary but you soon learnt the tactics. I discovered some simple rules that served me well. If you followed the etiquette properly you would be saved a night in the local hospital.

> *Rule One:* Don't enter first. Let some other plonker take the first battering. Better still, send in a muso virgin to take the first hit.
>
> *Rule Two:* Keep your elbows high and busy. If possible make them sharp, pointed and firm. That keeps a few of the smaller intruders away.
>
> *Rule Three:* Avoid the spilt beer. Not easy this one, but the chance of ending up on your arse with thirty soaking-wet skinheads and punks piling on top of you is dramatically increased if you slip.
>
> *Rule Four:* Be strong but don't overdo it with the Buster Bloodvessel twin. He's bigger than you, spends all day carrying bricks up scaffolds and, to be honest, only smiles when the judge says, 'haven't I seen you here before, Mr Vessel?'
>
> *Rule Five:* Get in and enjoy yourself. Oh, and don't wear glasses.

What people forget is that we musos are bonded together through the rite of music. It makes us all pals. And so if anyone does fall over there'll always be someone to pull you up.

'You alright mate?'

'Yep. Cheers mate.' Pleasantries completed, they then return to battering the hell out of each and everyone else *down the front*.

My first experience of being in front of the stage and in this war zone was watching the infamous Killing Joke.

Killing Joke made some punk bands look like, well, Manhattan Transfer. They were hard. Really hard. I remember them once being interviewed by Paula Yates on the excellent TV programme *The Tube*, when they were challenged about their attraction to violence… I can't precisely recall the reply but Geordie's smile clearly suggested they liked a good fight. Like a number of other punk bands, fighting was part of the deal and so it made being right down at the very front all part of the gig experience. My early exposure must have been seeing and feeling Killing Joke's tribal anthem track "Wardance." It became hypnotic. The tension and anger could be bottled. It was ferocious, frightening but at the same time thrilling.

I remember when Bob (a few years before his attempt on my life at the Reading Rock Festival) and I nervously crept up the concrete stairs of the Top Rank Club, Reading. We could smell the damp beer-stained carpet. Around us were a mixed gathering of spiked hair, no hair, black ripped jeans and mud-covered T-shirts screaming anti-government slogans.

I can't recall the support band. We decided to stay near the back until the Joke emerged. They opened their set with a roar. I vaguely recall them having two drummers, which quadrupled the noise and pulsating hypnotic rhythm. Jaz Coleman, the lead singer, looked as mad as we all thought he was. A fire-eater emerged on stage and added another ten degrees to the inferno. For over an hour we jumped, crashed and mashed each other. The place was a battlefield. No one spoke or smiled. We were in a trance. We knew all the tracks by the sound not the prose.

Bob and I survived. Whoever picked us up that evening must have died of shock. A few hours earlier two polite schoolboys had entered the seedy concrete extension to the bus station… a few hours later the same young boys reappeared wetter than if they had swum the Thames, smiles creeping out of their mouths and as deaf as two posts. We looked at each other unable to speak, but both knowing we had survived being down the front and we would never look back.

For this reason, I love standing.

Having survived Killing Joke, I pushed the boundaries and spent most of my first years gigging making sure I was down the front. It became a must-do. If you didn't get down the front you couldn't have had a good gig. How many times have you been asked or overheard people and mates leaving a venue, claiming rights as to how close they got to the stage? Come on, we've all been there.

Soaking wet T-shirts were the sign of a great night out. Those early years saw me regularly get close to the stage and my heroes. I remember in 1981 going to see the Gang of Four CND concert at the beautiful Rainbow Theatre. To this day I'm not really sure why I went – associating with a radical youth movement whose arguments, to be honest, I hadn't fully worked out if I was for or against. I was a teenager searching and, like all teenagers, a bit of rebellion was like learning English. The Gang of Four gig had one amazing benefit, besides it being a Friday: there was an unnamed special guest. As I waited for the headliners to emerge, the announcer arrived on stage, grabbed the central microphone and announced:

'Good evening everyone. Here are tonight's special guests…' – a short theatrical pause – 'The Jam!' I'm not sure how many people the venue held, it wasn't completely full, but suddenly there was an enormous surge forward. Everyone charged for the front. It was mental. The whole place shook to hundreds of pogoing youth.

The Jam provided one of the most compact and memorable support acts I have ever seen and will ever see. It was dreamlike.

More gigs followed fast. Reading Top Rank supplied me a reasonable share. The Damned, Level 42. The Undertones were excellent. We spent the whole gig pogoing to the classics such as "My Perfect Cousin," "Jimmy Jimmy" and my – along with many others of my generation – favourite track of all time, "Teenage Kicks."

Interestingly, Feargal Sharkey spent virtually the whole set sitting on the drummer's stand, with mic in hand, and hardly lifted his head. I would learn years later that this brilliant band was, like many, dysfunctional, and Feargal was on his own. But most of the real names had to be seen in London. Wherever we went it was the same. If we wanted to really experience and feel a part of the show we had to be down the front.

Yes, I'm a bit old now for the pit. And there's the trend of stage diving, which suggests you're likely to get your head kicked in by someone flying across the pit area about six feet off the floor with large walking boots on. I have to show my age and say I've never stage dived. Cowardice, age, weight; maybe I just don't see the point. I've scrambled on stage at a few early gigs but ended up with flapping arms and feet up in the air being dragged out at head height by very hacked-off security. I don't know why but I prefer a simple pogo or the odd 'wasp dance.'

Of course the beauty of standing is that you can choose where to stand and watch. You're not directed to a specific viewpoint where you must remain all night. You're free to move around, jig on the spot, avoid the tall git in front of you… he's always there. You can shuffle or if you need to, go for relief or get another round in. These last points are slightly tricky, as it means politely jostling through a crowd that is settled and nicely positioned. And having done whatever it was that you left your perfect viewing spot for… you have to find your way back.

For these reasons I have a policy of not leaving during a set unless there are exceptional circumstances. I certainly hate being pushed past by the drunken bloke who is attempting to carry three pints of venue lager and ends up spilling the remaining third over your shoulder.

Those experienced gig-goers in the know have developed some kind of terms of engagement. For one, always respect those that want to move past you. The exception being the totally pissed and those that grope or try to snog your girlfriend. They simply deserve a massive kicking. Usually, though, a smile and polite thank you is the key to safe passage. Smiling is very simple. After a while, things do sort themselves out. You *will* find that millimetre gap between all the heads in front and you *will* actually see the lead singer.

Some dear folk obviously do not quite get the etiquette of standing. I remember one gig in Cambridge – it was David Byrne from the fabulous Talking Heads. The crowd were mostly middle-aged or older. We were united, intrigued by Byrne and his remarkable talent, and keen to hear some classic Talking Heads tracks. Most of us had never seen him live before.

On this occasion I decided to head mid-stage near the front, about twelve rows back. We were standing of course. I thought it was a good spot for sound and viewing.

We took up our positions early. Some of us had beers in hand. However, just a row in front and to my right was this bloke who had clearly heard of Talking Heads but maybe only on the radio. I'll call him Mr C and A. He started to show signs of unfamiliarity with this standing thing. Something about him was different from the rest of us. He was quite tall. The big give-away was that he was wearing a smart shirt and jacket.

A couple of folk took the relief slot and ambled back to their original positions near the front. One muso just slightly caught Mr C and A's elbow as he brushed past. Mr C and A shot out a look of hatred as if someone just given his newly polished company car a small scratch. As the crowd quickly became quite packed, another brave but experienced muso entered what was apparently Mr C and A's own personal zone. Everyone was squeezing together, trying to get the best position. The experienced one bumped into him – it was impossible not to. Mr C and A had moved three centimetres but that was the last straw. He turned round to the muso and exploded with anger.

'Get off my spot!' he screamed.

'What?' asked the bemused experienced one.

'This is my spot. I'm standing here,' blasted Mr C and A.

'I can see that. Are you having a laugh? You didn't reserve it. This is the standing area. This is where people stand. If you want a reservation, then bloody well sit.'

If Mr C and A could have got his hands up, I'm sure he would have hit him. Luckily he couldn't. They eyeballed each other in a tense stand-off. I whispered to Jenny, 'that was brilliant. Did he expect to get a little reserved sticker marking his place on the floor? Dickhead.' I looked around and every other couple seemed to be whispering the same thing to their partners. We musos stick together.

David Byrne performed a sublime set. It was a night when we were treated to a musical masterclass by a pure genius. I recall the perfection to detail in every note. Byrne wanted everything to be perfect; luckily for us, it was. For Mr C and A ? To be honest, I didn't care. I hope he learnt his lesson and sits from now on.

These days I'm getting a bit more selective about going down the front. I expect it's my age. I'll still happily jump around to bands and tracks I love. In fact I gloat to myself when I see I'm the only one pogoing to one of my surviving heroes playing some B side not heard of – let alone performed – for 30 years. For the newer bands I smile at seeing the new generation of musos crashing about like mud wrestlers. I smile as I remember when I was young. 'Go on,' I say. 'Get down the front.'

For most of my gig-going career, getting down the front has been relatively safe. Yes, the odd elbow has been directed at a few vulnerable areas. Yes, I have entered the zone with teeth and fists clenched. I recall the Siouxsie and Banshees gig at the Hammy Palais in 1984 being pretty tasty. It had a larger-than-normal punk and skinhead gathering. Siouxsie seemed to be overtly tribal. The tension and hard rhythms intensified and the jostling became very aggressive. The pounding tracks such as "Nightshift," "Voices," "Happy House" and "Spellbound" were darker and extra heavy. But, as always whenever a muso falls over, someone would pull them up and shake them down. Only to go back in again.

I didn't think things could get much tougher down the front until, during my stay in Oxford, the infamous Killing Joke played one of the heaviest gigs I ever experienced. It was in our poly's main hall. Now, as you can expect, Killing Joke weren't every student's favourite act, even during the mid-1980s. So in place of many of my poly mates were the Oxford hardcore. In spite of the city's international renown, Oxford had a big posse of angry youth who *loved* bands like Killing Joke.

Stu was on stewarding duties but managed to get a shift at the back of the hall. At the front it was mayhem. The Joke were loud and raucous. The crowd were cold and needed warming up… and they got it. Jaz and the team were electric. I stood towards the middle, it just seemed too crazy to be down the front where every skinhead, punk and scumbag from miles around was jumping around as if on speed. They probably were. The front was a warzone. There were arms everywhere. The crowd surged from side to side. Every now and then a gap would form and then there would be a shuddering forward lunge of bodies.

But even this wasn't enough for some. A few mad souls decided that being down the front was simply not good enough. They wanted to be on the stage. At every chance, someone jumped up and clambered on. Our panic-stricken security mates, including my friend Alex, spent track after track pushing or carrying one of the mad souls off the stage. But back they came, again, again and again.

By half way through the set it was getting crazy and very dangerous. It was hard to concentrate on the excellent tracks belted out by this immense band. Suddenly one of the band's own security guys appeared to the side. He was a small guy and wore a country-style flat cap. One of the punks climbed back up – and the guy with the cap made his move. He rushed over to the stage invader, who was now grinning back at his pals, arms whirling around. Then in slow-motion the security guy raised a small truncheon and smashed it down right on to the fan's skull. He collapsed to the ground. He was out for a few minutes but the band played on, completely unmoved, ratcheting up the tension with every tribal beat.

The mad soul got up and was pulled into the pit at the front by his pals. He was now very angry. His pals saw it all – they charged the stage, this time from the side, exactly where Alex and a couple of our security guys were standing. All mayhem broke out. Fists and boots were flying in. It was carnage. Punches and kicks rained down… The band, though, carried on. The rest of the audience could only stand and watch. I was now frightened. This could get totally out of control. The music just fuelled the fire. The whole atmosphere was pure anger and hatred. "Wardance," "Requiem," "Follow the Leader" were like petrol on the fire.

Somehow the fight was stopped and the mad souls returned to the front. Killing Joke left the stage. Our ears were ringing, our eyes were out on stalks, our hearts were pounding. Thank God there were no knives.

A couple of days later I made my weekly trip to the local indie record shop on the high street. I was flicking through the racks of vinyl. In walked a local celebrity known as Peanuts. He was one of the mad souls and a recognised local nutter, hardcore. He was noticeable by his customary wearing of a dog collar. He was small, no more than five feet tall, with short thin white-bleached hair. He had a wicked smile, almost evil. I expect he hated students. He was noticeable everywhere as he had a large spider's web tattoo on his neck. He was hard, very hard.

But today he was different. Across his forehead was a large bandage. Upon entering the small shop he headed straight to the section of albums next to the wall, close to the counter, right next to me. The shopkeeper watched him carefully. Both of us knew the section being carefully handled. The cardboard divider displayed the letters JKL.

'Looking for Killing Joke, are you?' asked the shopkeeper, trying to engage with him.

'Did you see them at the Poly on Saturday?' the shopkeeper added, with a hint of nervousness.

'Yeah. It was fucking great,' replied Peanuts.

I slowly raised my eyes in astonishment. There I was, standing next to the guy who could have suffered brain damage on Saturday night; and here he was, saying how much he enjoyed the gig. *Unbelievable.* I was gobsmacked.

Nine: **Born Too Young**

I won't dance in a club like this
All the girls are slags
And the beer tastes just like piss

"Nite Klub" by The Specials

TIMING IS EVERYTHING. How often have we looked into our deeper soul and questioned why we missed something very special? Our 'if onlys' and 'what might have beens' are part of the story of our lives. In terms of music I bet we've all got bands on our hit list we'd do anything, almost, to see. Or maybe we were too young or couldn't afford the ticket or, even worse, lost the ticket or got ill the night before. I've missed my fair share of gigs even though I didn't think it was very fair at the time.

In my teenage, rebellious years I often felt really pissed off that my mum and dad left it so late to meet. Why couldn't I have been born in 1960 and not 1964? If I had been born just four years earlier I could have been allowed to see Led Zeppelin at Knebworth or Bob Marley at the Rainbow Theatre. I would have seen the Stiff Tour, punk at the height of its infamy, early versions of bands that became my heroes. But in 1980, being 16, shy and a bit of a coward, I didn't get to some legendary shows.

I guess I had a genuine excuse for missing these bands. I was either too young or they'd already overdone the booze and drugs. But the first band I could've seen but missed were actually alive and very well. I was in Oxford when this band were starting out, playing larger and larger venues, getting a bigger and bigger fan base.

'Are you going tonight?' Simon said while playing pool in the student bar.

'Who are you seeing?' I innocently replied. Our conversations were great. We both loved music and were regular gig reviewers for the Oxford Poly magazine, *The Last Edition*. I knew he wasn't talking about football – he never kicked a ball or did bingo – so it had to be a gig.

'They're playing tonight, here at the Apollo!'

'Who?' I asked again.

'The Smiths,' he said, as if I was from Mars.

'I haven't got a ticket.'

'We've got a spare,' he said.

'I'm not sure, Simon. I can't quite get my head around Morrissey's vocals.'

'Ok, it'll be great and they're going to be big, I mean *massive*.'

And so it was – apparently. I wasn't there. However I replay that time and that conversation I still get it wrong and don't go. Of course Simon was right. The Smiths by the mid-1980s were huge. Every student at the time – in their depressed, head-down, morose and sad way – was into them. I said no. I had turned down a ticket. I missed seeing them before they took over a generation. What a prat!

A few years later I heard "How Soon is Now?" It has one of the most brilliant contagious riffs ever, played by the excellent Johnny Marr. I went The Smiths mad. My only saving grace was that Nic's girlfriend at the time was writing an essay on Morrissey. One of her entertainment contacts had offered to set up a face-to-face meeting with the main man… but for some reason she said no. Phew, I thought. That's worse than my story. I was looking for excuses.

I was a huge Bob Marley fan at school – in fact I was probably his only fan there. We certainly didn't have any Rastafarians in my class, and the only connection with the West Indies was everyone's love of cricket: Curtly Ambrose and Joel Garner. It was probably my wretched independence and unknowing desire for non-conformity that sparked off my instant interest in reggae. It conjures up so many wonderful images and sensations. Blue skies, clear seas, sugar canes, rum and warmth. The problem was that, as I was starting out on my musical journey, the man most famed for making reggae internationally acceptable was dying of cancer.

I fell in love with all those wonderful reggae tunes such as "Three Little Birds" and "Stir It Up." *Uprising* was and remains one of the greatest albums ever made. It's a true classic, full of life, warmth and passion.

I've thought long and hard as to why I love reggae music. Maybe it's the strong rhythms, the clear stroking chords or the off-beat. It seems really simple, but that's wrong. Often the simplest song is the hardest.

I cried the day Bob Marley died. He was a legend. I wore a black tie to school, much to the sarcasm of friends and bemusement of the teachers. Most of the teachers hated rock 'n' roll and everything their narrow minds thought it represented. Not all my school chums were anti-reggae, but a lot of them simply hadn't yet opened up to music.

Marley did a few gigs in the UK during his brief life, but sadly these were before the start of my gigging adventures. Fortunately many excellent bands have followed in the wake of Bob Marley and his brilliant Wailers. Bands such as Black Uhuru, Steel Pulse, Gregory Isaacs and Aswad. Then there were the more unknown, specialist bands like U-Roy, Toots and the Maytals and Yellowman.

I made up for missing the man himself by seeing some of these superb reggae bands instead. During my time at Oxford Poly, probably due to John Peel and Annie Nightingale plugging the reggae genre on radio, we managed to attract some class acts such as the wonderful Steel Pulse and Clint Eastwood and General Saint.

With student life came the exposure to other musically related things, such as drugs. Now, I can't hide the fact that a few students at the poly were taking drugs, but it wasn't overtly heavy. There was a group, primarily involving my friend Simon, who had been exposed to the wilder side of middle class London. He was also well into reggae and we bonded quickly. In fact we developed a weekly pattern on a Wednesday afternoon, if there was no football, of meeting after lunch, sharing a spliff and heading into Oxford to scour the various city record shops. We'd buy a few new releases, head back to my first-year room and drift into the evening playing music and having a real laugh.

In the summer holidays of 1984, Simon invited me to the Sunsplash Festival. It was in 'sarrff' London at the Crystal Palace football ground next to the Sainsbury's car park. It was a purely reggae affair and attracted many of the top artists of the time. It sounded great. Spending a whole day in the sunshine, drinking Red Stripe, having a spliff and listening to the pumping rhythms of some of the best reggae acts at the time – wicked.

The event was excellent – from what I can remember. I recall the strong Jamaican beer, the air full of a sweet marijuana smell and lots of lovely people rocking to that famous reggae beat. There were some great artists, including Black Uhuru, the hero Dennis Brown and the more popular Aswad. It was like a trip through Trenchtown. The food stalls were serving jerk chicken and other Caribbean delights. The crowd were an eclectic mix of young, old and the very old. Dress code was simply casual, though there were plenty of loud shirts. The music was dominated by a heavy bass from the enormous sound system. Everyone was very mellow as we seemed to sway our way through this beautiful summer event on Palace's pitch.

Aswad were interesting. While a reggae band at heart, they played an important role in helping reggae become part of the musical mainstream. A number of their tracks, such as "Don't Turn Around," made it to the Top Ten. I still think their lesser-known track "Bubbling" is pure genius. According to my dad, though, I also had a rather strange link with them.

Many of the band members were born in London and schooled in the Notting Hill area. Notting Hill was a rough, hard place, where streets of high deprivation and wealth sat close to each other. My father spent over thirty of his working and commuting years there between the early 1960s and late 1990s, when at the wonderful age of 75 (as his firm had gone bust) he got made redundant. The company was called Alfred Franks and Bartlett – or, as we knew it, AFB. At this time it was a family business, an importer of cheap cosmetics, quality sunglasses from Italy, toys and so-called 'fancy goods.' I never knew what this meant, although I was occasionally allowed to rummage through the showroom and take home the odd sample.

AFB were located near Latimer Road, west London, near the tower blocks close to the Westway. The area was infamous in the 1970s and 1980s for being rundown and not a nice place to visit in the evening. In fact the famous squatters' house, the Apocalypse Hotel, which took the local council to the European Court, was just a few properties away. Dad and I would watch every episode of *The Sweeney* to see the car chase scenes filmed on the road outside the warehouse.

The warehouse manager Alf Buckthorpe was an old school friend of my father's. He was a scream. A lovely mild-mannered Londoner with a brilliant sense of humour. He was a true cockney with a wonderful voice. He used to sing on the pub circuit throughout the East End. I smile just thinking about him.

Anyway, my father recalled a story when Alf took on a young local lad as a warehouse assistant. A budding musician who needed to get a few quid together; his band were just starting out in the early 1980s and needed the cash to buy their kit. Within a few days the conversation had turned to music. Before you knew it, in the small warehouse office, and surrounded by cardboard boxes and delivery slips, the young black musician was strumming away on a guitar while Alf was singing his Sinatras off. I expect there weren't many deliveries that day.

My father never showed anywhere near the passion for music that I do but to this very day he remains adamant that this young, passionate and determined young lad was Brinsley Forde – the future lead singer of Aswad. And while Brinsley, who has been asked about it, denies it was him, I believe my father. I would love to have been there to see and hear these two people from such different worlds and backgrounds play their songs, united through a love of music.

But when it comes to bands missed, I have to say that Led Zeppelin was one I truly wanted to see. I missed this mega rock band by days. In 1979, at Knebworth House near Stevenage, Led Zep played their probable last-ever gig. A fitting place to go out. My cousin Marc, being a few years older than me and well into rock, did everything possible to skive off from the record shop in Bournemouth where he worked so he could go to the gig. He even drove to some unknown house to pick up a spare ticket from a complete stranger… There was no eBay in those days.

I was, though, just emerging from my protected world. Led Zep was on my radar but a gig near some new town north of London was a trip too far. Besides, I didn't have a ticket and I was only 15. The next year, the drummer, who had such an influence over my desire to pick up some sticks, drank himself to death. Led Zep disbanded. I was gutted. I would never hear "Kashmir" live.

Or would I? For reasons I don't know, Jimmy Page and Robert Plant decided in 1994 to get back together to produce an album called *No Quarter*. It wasn't a Led Zep reunion because John Paul Jones wasn't invited. But it was Page and Plant. The album itself was received well and I liked it, while accepting that it wasn't the real Zeppelin. Page and Plant decided to take the album on the road. Jez and I thought this was worth a trip to the Wembley Arena hangar.

Good job we did. You will know by now that, for me, a gig can be classed a success if a number of things come together. For example great sound, good light show, performers on top of their game. By this point on my journey I was building a huge repertoire of tracks that just made me *tingle*. One such song was (and is) "Kashmir." I've never been able to put my finger on it. I've had to play it again and again while writing just to get me it into the groove. It's one of the most powerful songs I've ever heard. The crashing twin bass drums, the rising violins and haunting Plant vocal. The track builds and builds, just like the journey in the song.

When recording *No Quarter*, Page and Plant decided to redo a number of their classics, including "Kashmir." The re-recording was stoked up with Middle Eastern influences; a real Middle Eastern orchestra added the mysticism and heat from this wonderful part of the world. The original was brilliant, but this new version took it – and me – into orbit. But what about it live?

Jez and I connected when it came to Led Zep. We were both hooked by their power, the complexity, the subtlety and divine vocals. We managed to get seats close to the side of the stage. There was no standing, but we knew we needed to be as near to the front and the band as we could. There was a huge roar when they appeared on stage and the house lights went out. Expectations were at fever pitch. Straightaway, Plant's vocal and Page's riff exploded, ripping through the venue. Jez and I looked at each other, grinning. This was what we had been missing.

Each track got stronger and stronger. There was a slight pause. Then came "Kashmir." Led Zeppelin had such an awesome sound but coupling it with an orchestra… well, there are few words to describe it. This was *No Quarter*'s strength. But to blow our minds tonight, they didn't have one orchestra – they had two. The live show included both an English *and* a Moroccan full-piece orchestra. I lost count of how many people were on the stage. But what came out of those numerous Marshall amps was simply orgasmic. As "Kashmir" started, this favourite track of mine, I went on another, *deeper* journey. The various strings lifted me into the stratosphere. Up and up I was taken. The track went on and on… I forget how many minutes passed. I didn't mind, it could go on forever for all I cared. I was lost, gone. Music had done its trick. My soul had left my body. I was blown away.

The track ended in a crash of drums, screams and strings. The place roared. I had never seen an audience explode. Had they all just felt what I had? Had we all been taken out of our skins and shown the magical door to musical eternity? I was crying. I could find no other way to let it out. As the final note faded away I turned to Jez. 'That's it, Jez.'

'What?' he asked, slightly blearily.

'That was the best track I've ever seen in my whole life. I don't need to see or hear anything ever again.'

There was one band I *was* old enough to see who, singlehandedly, created a new rage, a new style and definitely a new noise.

The late 1980s were a difficult era in music. The dance scene was still in its infancy, New Wave and the indie scene were parked in the sidings. While there was plenty of music around, we were looking for something new.

Over in the States things were changing. In the UK we started to hear about a band that were ripping up the script. It was led by Kurt Cobain, and the band was Nirvana. They were a revelation. They were everything that was not around. Their sound was a pure roar. Kurt's vocal was simply a scream. When I first heard "Smells Like Teen Spirit" it only took those first couple of scratchy guitar riffs and I thought 'Wow!'

Nirvana became an overnight sensation. Kids everywhere seemed to metamorphose… grunge had arrived. I expect that even Kurt and the band never knew what an influence they would have on a generation desperate for something to scream and jump about to. To wear ripped jeans, grow long hair and walk around as if kicked in the balls for just being there. The musical press were also in search of a new trend. I missed the band's first UK tour, also their apparently amazing set at the 1991 Reading

Rock Festival. But in 1992 they returned to headline at Reading and were by now a legend.

In 1994 Nirvana announced a return to England and planned a short tour, including a gig at Brixton Academy. I jumped at the chance but knew I was probably going to have to go alone. I remember opening the pre-stamped envelope, seeing the tickets and smiling. I was excited.

The gig was in May and I was settling into Cambridge. There was lots on. I was getting to know about full-time work. I was making new friends, finding new places to visit. Time flew past.

As we neared the date, I started playing *Nevermind* (Nirvana's superb second album) a lot, probably too much for my housemates. I loved it when everyone was out. I'd move the furniture in the small living room, carefully place the black vinyl on the record deck and turn up the volume.

Then, in the second week of April I read with horror that Kurt was dead. He had apparently shot himself. He was dead. The tour was off and I wasn't going to see one of the most influential bands of the decade. I was shocked, totally shocked. I've missed a few bands before, but this was different. I had a ticket. All I needed to do was get down to Brixton, go in, jump maniacally around, squeeze the sweat out of my T-shirt and then come home and tell everyone I had just seen one of the most influential bands in the world. But no. Kurt was dead and the tour was off. I felt confused, one part angry, the other depressed. All I was left with was a copy of the NME with Kurt staring back at me.

All I could say to myself was, 'bloody hell, why now?' Selfishly.

The late 1980s and early 1990s were an interesting – arguably *the* understatement of this book –time in music. The end of the 1980s saw a shift from four-piece guitar-dominated indie bands towards dance. It kind of started with the 'Aceeed' craze and then moved into house, trance. A number of brilliant new DJs came to the fore and stole the limelight. All this was helped by new big club venues, all-nighters and a more accessible drug scene.

I reckon that music takes on something new, a new scene, a new genre, when times are tough. Recessions are very damaging as they hurt so many, especially those less well off or without connections. Music is a way of venting anger and frustration. It becomes an opportunity for expression and often rebellion.

The Thatcher 1980s saw the development of a greed culture. The financial markets and stock markets took over. I recall seeing images of young inexperienced postgraduates openly boasting about their newly found wealth, drinking champagne while snarling at the growing crowds of homeless people. Then suddenly it all went tits up. In one day *everything* was simply thrown in the air.

One day in the late 1980s I woke up to go to work, thinking that my new investment in a shared house was a great idea and would enable me to retire early, only to return that very evening to see that the value of our newly purchased house had fallen off a cliff. This was hard to understand, especially as there aren't any cliffs in Cambridge.

Dance was the new music. Large clubs playing mixed and sampled music with heavy rhythms and vibes. I was immediately drawn to this new emerging sound. Soon I was discovering a range of brilliant DJs who had perfected the art of transforming tracks – often classic hits in themselves – into songs you couldn't help but move to. The record label Perfecto and its many partners was a great pull, and soon I was discovering artists such as Paul Oakenfold, Pete Tong and Sasha.

A number of great places were emerging but I simply couldn't find the time or space to go. Cream was a sensation. The Ministry of Sound and the Hacienda were rammed. But I was never there. I never got in the door with the thousands in the hands-in-the-air posse. I never got covered in foam, never spent hours screaming, 'whoa, whoa,' blowing whistles or letting klaxons off.

While happy to pop along to gigs on my own, my main excuse was that the dance and club scene revolved around taking various forms of drugs with lots of mates. While not naive or prudish about drugs I was never into ecstasy, and neither were my gig-going mates. I knew people that were, but they were in established crews that spent virtually every weekend at some big club. I'm not mocking it, just noting that I never got there. Ken and I always plan to do our Ibiza thing at some stage… maybe. Maybe one day.

Anyone from the past four generations would have heard of it, certainly relate to it, probably seen a clip of it and maybe even have been there. Arguably the most significant campaign ad and charity event *ever* was held on Saturday, 13 July 1985. The main venue was the historic Wembley Stadium, though it was also held in the USA at the JFK Stadium, Philadelphia. The event was Live Aid.

The mid-1980s was a strange time. There was so much going on. In the UK we were mid-way through the Thatcher era; for many of us society was divided. Those who had got more; those unable to participate were marginalised. While those in the City were making mega cash, sipping champagne at lunchtime and stepping over an increasing number of rough sleepers on the way to the opera, others were struggling with the lack of jobs, clampdowns on benefits and less income.

In Africa things were even worse. Parts of this vast continent were suffering another but even more deadly famine. The issue of poverty in Africa had been noted before but this year in particular it was even more serious. People were dying in their millions. It didn't seem right. Michael Buerk did a harrowing report about it in a BBC programme in October 1984.

Bob Geldof of the Boomtown Rats picked up on it. He decided that the poverty, famine and corruption in Africa needed exposure. Following a series of visits to the squatter camps of Ethiopia he returned to a self-centred and complacent UK. While many of us indulged in lavish lifestyles and spent money on trivia – was his blunt message – there were some thirty million people dying and we were doing nothing about it. This was wrong, so wrong.

Working with Midge Ure, they produced an anthem song that should be in everyone's iPod, iPad, YouTube, iTunes database and record collection. "Do They Know It's Christmas?" was released on 25 November 1984 and rightly became the Christmas number one single. Suddenly we were all reunited. We had an issue. We had a cause. We were sad. We were angry. We cried. I remember hearing the song the first time and buying two copies to show my solidarity.

Through his tenacity and determination, Geldof had suddenly grabbed media and public attention. His and Midge's song involved a multinational collective of bands, singers and songwriters. It raised over £8 million. The single released under the Band Aid name consisted of virtually every famous musical has-been and wannabe. Everyone, now, wanted to be involved. Those not associated with it were publicly humiliated by Bob. And we the public also felt the guilt. We wanted to care and give something back. Buying the single was a simple but direct way of showing empathy.

Bob then came up with the mad dream of putting on a global event to change the world. Live Aid. A live gig in two countries at the same time. Now madly into music and gigging, the opportunity to attend such an important event was well and truly on my radar. But I had a problem. My old school had planned to hold a reunion summer ball, its first, on Saturday, 15 July 1985. The same bloody day as Live Aid. To be fair the ball had been planned well in advance of the Live Aid date being announced. I had tickets already, and I knew my first love was going.

Live Aid tickets went on sale in various locations across the land. They were sold in person and you had to queue. I was in a dilemma. I had paid for tickets to Bradfield's ball. I wanted to be there, I wanted to be with my friends, I wanted and needed to see Fiona. But. But there was this gig. A gig with so many leading and famous bands. It would be a one-off. Surely I should go?

I honestly regret my decision. It pains me even today. I chased a past dream. I turned down the gig the world would see and remember for decades.

I remember driving from Oxford to Reading on the Live Aid day. I listened to the preparations on the radio in ERD and arrived home just in time to see Status Quo open the event with "Rocking All Over the World." As soon as this track started playing I realised my mistake. I knew I should have been there. For the next five hours I was glued to our TV. I hardly spoke to mum and dad, who I hadn't seen for over three months.

I'll never forget Bono performing "Bad" and climbing down to the crowd and pulling out that young girl and dancing with her at the foot of the stage. Absolutely brilliant. I, with millions of others, was glued to the screen. We cried and cried. In the background Bob was sitting with Prince Charles and Lady Diana, screaming out, 'give us your fucking money.'

I genuinely could have been there. A friend from Oxford Poly went. He queued up at the Apollo and got tickets. I could have done that. Instead I missed the most famous gig on earth ever.

If there was any consolation I was lucky to win tickets to the Live 8 gig held in Hyde Park on 2 July 2005. This also had an amazing line-up. But I'll always regret not going to see Live Aid. I can only ask that if you haven't ever watched anything from the event, *do*. Get the DVD or video and watch it.

Ten: **Venues**

I, I will be king
And you, you will be queen
Though nothing will drive them away
We can be Heroes
Just for one day

"Heroes" by David Bowie

I HATE SHEDS. Not the one in my garden of course. One day I'll transform this little wooden shack into a music temple-cum-studio. A musical tardis. I'll have it all wired up with my Bang and Olufsen surround-sound system so I can lock myself away to drown in the music I love. I think the plants might like a bit of Cocteau Twins as they start their precious, short lives.

Anyway back to the plot. When I say 'sheds' in a musical context I mean those huge buildings, such as Wembley Arena, in which so many bands, having allegedly 'made it,' end up entertaining us. Of course we also have the mighty hangars such as Earls Court and O2 Arena, or Dome as it once was. I respect that a band wants to play large venues. Why wouldn't they? It's not just about the huge income. I'm sure any band yearns to play their music to the biggest possible number of people in the largest possible space. But for some bands, playing huge venues is risky. For many it just does not work.

Hangars and sheds go against a muso's *raison d'être*: you want to get intimate with the band, their music and the whole show thing. Unless you take specific measures you lose everything that makes a good gig, for one simple reason: usually you're bloody miles from the band. Nic's mate Julian takes binoculars to see gigs in sheds. What's the point? To make matters worse, the sound in these corporate cash registers can be shocking. Even my basic physics tells me that sound, within a large enclosed space, takes a long time to reach both the ceiling and the back. The result is a horrible echo. And there's the time lag. If you're at the back of a hangar you can be so far out of time with the band that they're well into the next song before you've had a chance to applaud the first.

On my gig-going journey the venue issue has created a huge dilemma for me. Many of my favourite bands have gone on to be extremely successful – in some cases, world famous. Along with the fame they end up playing larger and larger venues: the corporate sheds and hangars. Too often I've had to weigh up a few issues. Firstly, should I be bothered to go or not? Then, what if I can't get a standing ticket? Do I risk being seated high up in the Gods, right on the edge of the doubtfully safe raised tier, looking down on the five-a-side football pitch below where people look smaller than Subbuteo figures?

In my early gig-going years this wasn't so much of an issue. I would always choose to stand at gigs, it was built into my DNA. But when I was youthful and learning my trade I simply wanted to see bands. I was an apprentice. A student of 'music venue attendance.' Being at the gig was more important than being snooty over whether I sat or stood. In my formative years I spent lots of time attending gigs in London. Many were at the famous Hammy Odeon or even that shed of all sheds, Wembley Arena, where I quite often had no choice but to buy seated tickets.

The problem with Wembley is the same today as it has always been. It's a pig to get to and even worse to get home from. I've always thought that the location of Wembley Arena and Stadium is some national conspiracy sponsored by the local council and the London Underground. It's a pain. At times, though, getting there can be fun, especially if it's for a big band or big match. The tube to Wembley is perfect for raising the excitement levels, joyful banter and some relatively contained winding up of the opposition.

But how many of us have endured that horrid, crowded, depressing journey home? Your team has lost, the ref was blind and the defence had more leaks than Thames Water. If you aren't quick about leaving a show or match, you end up being herded like cattle all the way to the tube. The last thing you need. Then you take your life in your own hands as you stand on an overcrowded Wembley Park station waiting for a tube to hurtle in. Of course connection times rarely work, and there's the real threat you'll miss the last train home. So in the early years I used to drive to gigs at Wembley.

Looking back to the early 1980s, I've been quite lucky really. The battle between the desire (in the red corner) to see a band and the perfection (in the blue corner) of the event was easily won by desire (by a knockout). I saw some great names both new and old in my foundation years. Bands such as Roxy Music, Santana, Depeche Mode and, probably the best at this time, The Police. Most of these gigs were sufferable seated affairs. We were politely directed to our seats by stewards in orange hi-vis jackets. No sooner had the house lights been extinguished than everyone was standing and cheering. All good fun, unless you dared to try and move anywhere out of your allotted space. 'No way, Jose.' The kind-faced hi-vis jacket became a zealous security guard and would immediately direct you back to your seat – politely, of course.

Alternatively you could just smash up your seats and have a riot – which Nic and a few thousand other Rainbow fans did in 1980 when Ritchie Blackmore and his band only played a short set and refused to come back for an encore. Tetchy, these heavy rock fans.

After a couple of visits to the Arena and clocking the seriousness with which these volunteer security guards plied their trade, I devised a little plan to get closer to the stage. Before the start I would stand a bit higher up and try to spot the odd empty seat at the front. After Track Three I would chance my luck. This neat trick was helped a few years later when an Oxford Poly friend turned out to be one of these hi-vis-clad volunteers. At the U2 gig in June 1987 I took a punt and bought tickets on the side. For some reason U2 weren't able to offer a standing section. I identified myself to my hi-vis-clad pal, who disappeared downstairs. Within a few minutes he was back and beaming. He had kindly sussed out a few empty seats down on the arena floor near the front. After the famous Track Three we were, rather like royalty, escorted down to the front. Wicked! I took my final exams the next day and passed. It must have been worth it.

Over the years I've nurtured that internal battle between desire and perfection. Things have changed over time. I've become much more discerning when considering seeing bands in sheds or hangars. For now, I strictly only attend if I can stand. Perfection: up on points. I know that standing enables me to get close and I can use my years of gig-going tactics to find that unobstructed viewing spot. But most importantly it creates the pretence of the intimacy I normally find in a smaller venue. Once in this 'down the front' zone and the band are strutting their stuff, I can forget the travel nightmares and the appalling echo. To be fair, at least we now have sufficiently qualified sound engineers to overcome the challenges of these vast halls.

The pursuit of perfection became truly embedded in my gig-going philosophy a few years back when I went to see Duran Duran at the O2 Arena. I was on one of those nostalgia trips, seeing another band on a reunion tour. Duran Duran had managed to keep themselves relatively together over the decades and still turn out a good pop song. Many of their contemporaries, though, have either faded away or the band members couldn't hold back their hatred of each other; or alcohol and drugs took them to that huge jukebox in the sky. Duran Duran have survived.

I quite like the O2, as a building. The Lord Rogers design is unique as architecture. The white roof material is unimaginably light, hung like a Bedouin tent off twelve 100-metre yellow poles that stick out like knitting needles. I didn't get to see the millennium show, and when Crisis (the charity I work for) held their Christmas do, there I was too busy with a new and growing family to go along. Perversely, I was pleased when the venue was saved and turned into a kind of out-of-town entertainment zone. It made good sense – even better when the Jubbly-Jubbly Line was extended to reach it.

The problem was simple. The main arena is huge. The ceiling rises some fifty two metres from ground level and disappears into a black void. The ticket agents even warn you not to buy tickets at the higher levels if you're afraid of heights. Unbelievable! I get vertigo just looking at the booking form.

Duran Duran meant a lot to me. In those early 1980s I was developing my interest in everything musical I had signed up as a gig-going apprentice at precisely the same time as the New Romantics stormed the charts and then the world. I can claim that every muso friend of mine has a copy of their self-titled debut album. That brilliant piece of white art, neatly emblazoned with their name in red and a band photo. For some rash reason I decided to see what they were like many years after their brilliant Hammy Odeon venture in 1981, my seventeenth gig. The only tickets I could get were half way back on the side and half way up. There was no health warning on the tickets, which was slightly reassuring… though there should have been. It should clearly have said: '*This event, for which you've paid a shedload of cash, will be attended mainly by middle-aged couples, who, for this night, have arranged for Granny to look after the youngsters, and are not a true representation of your typical hardcore muso.*'

Many co-attendees were probably on their own nostalgia trip but probably hadn't seen a band live for years. And definitely not been down the front. Maybe some thought it would be a fun night out, or just wanted to hear the old hits live for one more time. Surely even they couldn't have enjoyed the corporate wallet-pinching exercise you find in these sheds and hangars? To be fair, Duran Duran played a reasonable set, but it was a gig devoid of any intimacy, a gig of echoing sound and expensive piss-beer. I felt constrained in my seat and spent more time watching the couples trying desperately to dance and enjoy themselves. Many seemed more intent on sending texts or recording the odd track on their iPhone while shaking their arms around. I'd like to have seen them replay that to their mates.

That was it. The gig attendance committee met shortly after this event and declared a major policy decision. It was agreed that from that day I would now only be allowed to go to sheds and hangars in exceptional circumstances and upon the production of an independently validated argument – unless of course, I was able to get a standing area ticket. As the Crown Prince of England, played by Hugh Laurie, would say: 'Hurrah for democracy with knobs on!'

The Duran Duran gig was the tipping point. A serious point of no return.

Over the years, my abhorrence of the larger venues was probably building up to a crisis. The classic mother hangar of all hangars is Earls Court. I had experienced Earls Court in my youth when it was destination of one of those annual family days out… a trip to London to see the Ideal Home Exhibition. Here you could see the homes of the future, constructed in their entirety. They actually had fully sized homes erected in the main arena fully fitted with everything from the large double bed to the doll's house.

Earls Court seems to have become the ultimate indoor venue for those bands that claim to have made it. It's the one venue they will boast about playing in for ever and ever and ever and ever. For many it was their 'I played there' moment.

Led Zeppelin set the scene by playing five nights there in 1975 – many say these were their best ever performances. And tickets cost between £1 and £2.50.

'Yeah, man, we filled that place and blew the fucking roof off, man.' If only they had.

Now, before I get barred for life from such venues, I can report that I *have* witnessed a few exceptional shows there. Two of them were performed by one of those great bands that such hangars may even have been designed for. In 1980 Pink Floyd brought out their epic-scale album *The Wall*. The staging needed so much room that Earls Court was probably the only venue to have this live show indoors.

Back in 1980, my internal desire-versus-perfection debate hadn't started. And this event was simply a no-brainer. At the time it was marketed as the 'Only Ever Live Show of *The Wall*,' although no doubt its tremendous success made sure it was unashamedly repeated the following year. I got tickets but found myself near the back about half way up. As things turned out, I didn't need to worry. Along with Pink Floyd's huge global success, they'd picked up a truly professional team of lighting and sound engineers. Somehow they managed to pull off the impossible. We watched as an astonishing wall of huge blocks was built around Gilmore, Waters et al. There were monster puppets and crashing planes. And as for sound quality, each note was perfectly balanced, giving you the feeling of sitting at home in your comfy chair with headphones on. It was a masterclass in acoustics and how to put on a stage show. I was impressed. We all came away speechless.

In 1994 Pink Floyd, minus Roger Waters, were back. I was lucky – David Gilmour was a huge supporter of the homeless charity Crisis, of whom I was a trustee, and we were offered the chance to buy tickets on the arena floor a few rows from the front. I took my friend Ali, who – for an armchair fan – was as crazy about Floyd as you could get. By now I had formed a strong view about sheds and hangars and had started to play the desire-versus-perfection game.

The offer of good seats made it an easy choice. I also knew that Gilmour and team wouldn't let us down.

As the auditorium slowly filled up there was an amazing sense that you weren't at Earls Court but in a small private theatre. There was the polite chatter you get at theatres, but behind this you could hear and even feel a noise washing around the vast arena. It was like the sound of a wave rushing up the beach, drifting slowly from speaker to speaker. The sound steadily grew as we waited for lights out. As the crowd got bigger I noticed the backing sound increased.

'Ali, can you hear that sound?' I asked.

'No,' she said.

'Listen.' She did. 'Oh yes, what is it?'

'It's a kind of humming. It must be the sound desk playing with us. That's brilliant. I think we're in for a great gig.'

And we were. The Pink Floyd show was immaculate. Every note and every beat was perfectly in tune and rhythm. You started to wonder whether it was all pre-recorded and we were simply swimming in our own fish bowl.

While Pink Floyd had restored my dwindling desire for hangars, Prince and his mob destroyed it. Prince is a genius guitarist. He appeared to take over the world in 1985, becoming the superstar of superstars. To be honest I wasn't a mega fan, but I was curious. Was this man as good as his critics said? I decided to see him and his show. And that was what I got. A show. Not a gig. Yes, it was a highly choreographed performance. But there was none of the rawness I like at a real gig, no slight mistakes, no missed notes. Thanks to my position the echo wasn't noticeable, but neither was much else. In fact I was bored. Except for his purple suit and highly crafted guitars I came away with hardly any memories.

Arguably this wasn't Earls Court's fault. Prince was a genius, a mega star, but for me nothing happened. He tried, the sound engineer tried, but it simply didn't work. And this reaffirms my point: gig-going, seeing bands live, is a complex experience; so many factors need to come together to create that ultimate event. Bands playing in sheds and hangars have to work so much harder to make it memorable.

I've stood at Earls Court since. Now, if there was ever a band with egos that needed two Earls Courts, one each for its famous brothers, it was Oasis. There are miles and miles of newspaper and music press coverage devoted to the band that tried to put the 'Great' back into Britain in the 1990s. I have to say I was awestruck when I first heard them. I can recall to this day flicking through the vinyl in Selectadisc Records in London, August 1994, when *Definitely Maybe* burst out of the speakers. "Columbia" blew my mind.

'Who on earth is that?' I enquired at the desk.

'Oh, it's the new album from that Manchester band, Oasis. Good, ain't it?'

'I think it's excellent. Just what music has been missing for the past few years,' I offered.

I bought the lovely gatefold sleeve album – it rarely left my decks for four months before I saw them at the Cambridge Corn Exchange in December. Jump forward three years, and it seemed that every muso in the world had heard of Oasis and the machinations of the Gallagher brothers. By 1997 the Britpop battle had ended – I admit I loved both Oasis and Blur, but for very different reasons.

Now, Earls Court is huge, and so is Liam Gallagher's head. So it was fitting that Oasis would take the place over for a triumphant party. The great news was that the main arena was designated a standing zone. (Bands who do this stay true to their roots and followers.) Ken and I got our standing tickets and, after a couple of pints in the local crowded hostelry, headed in.

There was angst in the air. The crowd was mostly young men full of beer and vodka shots, out for an evening of loud music and fighting. Ken is a member of the down-the-front club too, and we immediately headed to the barriers. Already the crowd were swaying, and you could scrape the tension off the ceiling… Well, you would have done in any other venue.

Richard Ashcroft's The Verve provided an excellent, egomaniacal support act. They put in a great set, which included the flowing "Lucky Man" and "Bitter Sweet Symphony."

The house lights went out to a huge roar. We waited and waited. As if it was scripted, Noel and Liam kept us waiting. When they finally appeared the roof lifted off. Liam shuffled to the front and asked us if we were all 'mad for it.' For the next hour and a half we jumped around, bashing into anything and anyone next to us. Dripping with sweat we screamed out the hits… everyone knew all the words. It was a truly great gig. Oasis seemed to have brought all the young musos together. Putting city rivalries and football allegiances aside, we rock 'n' rolled.

I also learnt a very important lesson at this gig. By now my eyesight did not meet the requirements of the DVLA – I needed glasses to make sure I could actually see what I was looking at. Reluctantly, I'd had to come to terms with this form of ageing when I'd been to watch a footy match. As the players emerged from the tunnel, Lou turned to me and said, 'cor, have you seen Wrighty's new haircut?'

I looked hard at the ten men running towards our away end wearing red shirts and then turned to him (Oh, by the way, I *can* count. Our goalie wore yellow and I knew who he was):

'Er… I have a slight problem.' I paused for a moment. 'Which one is Wrighty?' My embarrassed reply wasn't out of ignorance, just blurred distance vision.

Glasses were the only option. I had to face it, this was the only way I could actually see… er, anything, and especially bands. The problem is, when down the front at a rock gig, wearing glasses isn't recommended. Pogoing is great but highly risky. Half way through the Oasis set, I was clipped by a flailing arm and my glasses fell to the floor. It's at these moments that the world goes into slow motion while my heartbeat, already at full throttle, goes into turbo. I panicked. Of course it made the situation worse. The place was heaving. It was also very dark and I – literally – couldn't see…

I bent down and formed an arch and fumbled around amongst the boots of my fellow gig-goers. It felt like forever, but must have been only twenty seconds. I pushed someone and then miraculously felt something and picked it up. It was my glasses and they were all in one piece. I swore to myself more in relief than anger. I couldn't believe how lucky I had been. I decided to watch the rest of the gig in a blur. Very ironic, I thought to myself.

Outside, Ken and I exchanged our first thoughts. Our heads were thumping. It had been a very, very loud gig. My ears rang for days afterwards. We agreed it was a great gig, very intense and a proper jump around. I told Ken about the glasses and we agreed I was very lucky, very lucky. Maybe I should get some contact lenses? I thought of Richard Ashcroft's song… I was that Lucky Man.

The Oasis gig had given me a battering in many ways. My

ears were pretty smashed, I nearly lost my glasses, after pogoing for nearly two hours my calves were killing me, and my back was covered in bruises from all the likely lads bashing into me while down the front. This was not your typical hangar experience. I expect many of those seated in the clouds couldn't even *imagine* the way I felt. The Oasis gig challenged my anti-hangar theory. It proves that even in a hangar you can experience an excellent gig if you take a punt and join in.

We're blessed in the UK. Not only do we have – and have had for decades – such a vibrant music scene, we also have some of the best venues in the world. Now, I'm saying this without having even started my global venue study tour. When I've been away I've recced a few places but still conclude we have the best range of venues anywhere. What's certain is that the venue is a key component of the whole gig-going thing. Wrong venue, the higher the risk of a poor show.

So let me take you to a few of my favourites.

The Junction in Cambridge has to be an all-time favourite venue. I moved to Cambridge in 1987 to take up a research job, putting my tour of the world on hold. Cambridge was great fun and good for my professional career. It was also a job that paid good money and took me to a part of the country I knew little about, but where I have since happily settled.

But in 1987 music venues in East Anglia were very few and far between, certainly good ones. There was the refurbished Cambridge Corn Exchange – this has provided a good source of bands over the years. But if you get a deaf sound engineer or one who thinks max 11 is best, then there's no chance of you hearing a good gig. Fortunately there have been a few notable exceptions, which I'll come to.

Anyway, in making my move across country to 'the other place,' what I didn't know beforehand was that I was arriving at a time of local rebellion. The local musos were demanding something new, somewhere smaller and more intimate than the Corn Exchange but larger and more music focussed than the Boat Race on Norfolk Street. The latter was a terrific venue and should not be dismissed. A number of friends, including Lee's ex-wife Jo, apparently saw Oasis play there! As a music venue the Boat Race was simple in intent: brilliant for folk bands, emerging bands and music that needs subtlety and intimacy. It was also a midweek place for meeting pals, drinking beer, chatting and straining to listen to a small group of musicians with bleeding fingers and stretched vocals. Sadly it closed in the 2004 and is now a restaurant. I miss it.

My arrival in Cambridge was very well timed. The local muso campaign had gained real momentum and resulted in a new venue as part of a cinema, bowling alley and restaurants development on the old cattle market. On 14 February 1990 – how romantic – the Junction was officially opened. The special opening night celebration featured some local bands, including The Cherry Orchard, supporting local boy Boo Hewerdine's The Bible. My housemates Jez, Rob and I got tickets. It was fun going into a new place.

The Junction is simple in form. The main auditorium is nicely compact. The wall blocks are painted black. The stage is sited in the corner to give maximum width. Originally it only had one bar selling a small range of beers but it did include Red Stripe on tap. The loos were simple, industrial metal. The place was clearly built to a low budget, but I didn't care. My journey wasn't about visiting good buildings – I could do that as part of my other life. For me it was a new place to hear live music and have a laugh.

The first night was absolutely brilliant. It was a real treat and privilege to have been there. Having just been recently released from that cushioned poverty trap of being a student, I immediately felt at home. (Of course students of my generation got grants not loans. We all left college bankrupt through our own mismanagement and not as a result of state policy). The Junction, while new, smelt and felt like a student hall – but this student-type venue was a million miles better than anything Cambridge University offered. With my student lifestyle still coursing in my veins, I hit the bar – and hard. The crowd were a mixture of local musos, music hacks and local celebs. Jez, Rob and I felt very special being there. We were interviewed by the local press and shouted loudly how great it was to have another venue in Cambridge. This first night had a real party feel – everyone was mixing, chatting, laughing and steadily getting very drunk. The beauty of smaller venues, especially those in the back rooms of small pubs, is that you can get a decent pint. What a treat. Here in Cambridge was not only a new, larger venue but also one that served good beer and strong lager. Yippee.

Local band The Cherry Orchard played a great, neat set. Their guitarist Jason would a few years later end up playing against our Sunday league footy team, the mighty Zebra. The drummer Chris got married to my housing friend Ruth. The headliners were The Bible – by the late 80s they had already established themselves on the scene. While at Oxford Poly I had seen them support China Crisis and found out that two of the band members were great mates with Nic, all three coming from Beckenham. Another footy pal, Dave Larcombe, was the drummer and one of the established local Mill Road drinking crew. It was turning out to be one big house party.

At some point The Bible took the stage and performed a solid, folky set based around Boo's unique vocal and seamless chords. By now I'd had far too many Red Stripes, and everything was starting to sway. I was so wrapped up in the music I didn't realise until the next day what these pints of strong lager had done. How we managed to get home I've no idea.

The next day was a work day, so I was up early and headed off. Only a few miles down the road the Red Stripe devil opened my head, got out her largest hammer and started to bang very hard. Inside my dumb skull was the hangover from hell. I went home and called in sick. When I emerged later in the day I thought what a brilliant night and a fantastic venue – I couldn't wait to go back.

Faithful to this promise, I often go back. Luckily the venue has survived, even expanded. It still attracts a superb range of artists. I feel very privileged to have such a great venue so close to home. The list of bands I've seen here is incredible. I feel spoilt. Every town should have one. For me it's 'our' Junction.

They celebrated their first birthday with a party, again on Valentine's Day 14th February 1991. The lovely exotic African Bhundhu Boys headlined with Lost T-Shirts of Atlantis in support. Now, I like a party, especially one where there's good music and very drinkable beer. To make it even more exciting the venue management decided to say thanks to everyone who'd been there on the opening night. The advert said that anyone with the original ticket stub could get in free. Brilliant, I thought. Of course I had kept mine. So the three of us trotted down for another potentially excellent evening –maybe not so many Red Stripes this time.

I boldly strolled up to the door staff. A young woman politely asked to see my ticket. I showed them my immaculate one from the first night.

'And what's this?' she said, bemused but smiling. They always smile at the Junction, even the security folk.

'Oh, it's the ticket from last year,' I replied.

'So?' Her smile was waning.

'Well, your advert said that anyone with a ticket stub from the opening night could get in free. Here's mine from last year. So can I go in, please?' I suggested calmly, logically, trying to keep smiling.

'Hey, John *(not his real name)* – is that true? Anyone with last year's ticket stub can get in for free?'

John thought hard. There was a long pause. 'I suppose so. I think we did say that somewhere. I thought it was a joke.'

'Well, if we said it, then fine. He can go in.'

With this resolved, I walked in. 'Oh, can I keep the ticket please? I collect them,' I asked in all seriousness. I must have been the only one to have taken up their generous offer. Twenty years later I was talking about this with the manager Edmund, who was collecting stories for the Junction's 20th party. I still had the ticket so I sent him a copy, apparently giving the current staff a good laugh.

I confess that my favourite medium-sized venues are in London. Hammy Odeon is like the place where you learnt to swim, Brixton Academy where you had your first snog, Wembley Arena where you ended up on your first trip to an out-of-town hardware megastore.

My gig-going travels have taken me to many wonderful places. Arguably – I bet this will cause loads of debate and conversation – I think three stand out. The first has to be one of the most famous venues in the world: the 100 Club on Oxford Street in London. Every city will have its iconic venue. I was in the converted Manchester Free Trade Hall for a conference this year with Keith. We were debating the merits of its place in the history of Madchester and the origins of punk. We concurred it would have been amazing to have been to some of those gigs there.

It's a scary time finally leaving education and entering the world of work, suits, daily routines, pay cheques, weekend sessions, gigging in real venues. Most of my college pals headed into London to start their careers. I had zipped off to Cambridge... on my own. Weekends were when we'd all meet up. Typically these would involve drinking and dancing. Even if not having a gig, the famous 100 Club used to hold a range of events on Fridays and Saturdays. For months we almost became weekend members.

I knew of the venue's fame and notoriety. This small underground place, with its dark walls, beer-covered carpet and low ceiling, was off Oxford Street down a narrow set of steps. At the bottom was the tiniest of kiosks where you'd pay your entrance money and pick up a ticket. I was too young to have got anywhere near in its punk hey-day, so I never saw any bands there when I was starting out – which I deeply regret.

But the post-punk era had profoundly taken me over. The Cure, The Undertones, Killing Joke, Simple Minds, Bauhaus, and Siouxsie and the Banshees. It's well documented that Siouxsie Sioux was there when it all took off in the mid- to late 1970s – those wild nights when the Sex Pistols stole the rule book, scrawled graffiti over it and then ripped it up in full public view. I missed all this. So when Siouxsie announced she would return to that very venue to celebrate her thirtieth year, I thought, 'I'm having that.' I couldn't stop smiling when the ticket arrived.

I suppose it's age or a weakening of the soul or a yearning for youth, but from the mid-1990s I found myself getting increasingly more emotional when it came to music. On the night of Siouxsie's return to the 100 Club I was in early. Very early. I stood at the bar, suddenly overwhelmed by gushes of emotion. Here I was, many years later, in the tiny club where so much amazing music was conceived. It was here, live on this very stage. And the woman there at this Holiest of Births was going to perform at snogging distance…

I sent a text to Stuart and Ken. It was a rambling message full of bollocks.

Stuart sent a profound and supportive reply. Ken just said 'Twat.' I knew what they both meant.

The lights went out and on marched Siouxsie and Budgie. On stage was a perfectionist Siouxsie with her bright black hair, wonderfully contrasted by Budgie with his scatty white peroxide mop. They gave the performance of their lives. Siouxsie commanded and patrolled the stage to military perfection. We even brushed palms as she caressed her adoring fans. This wasn't a show of greatest hits. I didn't complain. This one night brought it all together. The intimacy of the historic venue, the power of the raging music, the drive of Siouxsie's vocal and haunting sound… it gelled. And I really was there – though thirty years late.

Old cinemas are excellent venues. It's hard to put my finger on it but there's something quite special about these places. It's a really hard call as to a favourite. Even with the sad loss of the Astoria on Tottenham Court Road, there are still plenty to choose from. After much deliberation I have to say that the Town and Country Club (now the HMV Forum) in Kentish Town probably wins by a photo.

To me it will always be the Town and Country Club. It's one of those ritual things that you remember what a place is called the first time you go there. The first time I went was in 1986, to see Buddy Curtess and The Grasshoppers. It was called… surprise, surprise… the Town and Country Club. Good, that's got that straight.

It's in north London's Kentish Town, now the home of many lawyers, marketing execs and fashion designers. Back then it was a tough area dominated by students, artists and plenty on benefit. It had an edge, which in many ways, like the Rainbow, added to the excitement of seeing a band. It helped get the adrenaline going. Got you a bit pumped up.

The building itself was built in 1934 and has a wonderful art deco frontage. After the cinema closed it became a centre (serving the large local Irish community) for Irish dancing. In the 1980s it became a 2000+ gig venue. Although both ownership and name have changed, it remains an important music venue. It's smaller than, for example, the 5000-capacity Brixton Academy – that helps to keep the sense of intimacy. The lobby and foyer area is simple. Stairs on either side go up to the huge balcony seated area; two dark double doors lead to the back of the stalls. This is typically a dark area, enclosed by the balcony above. Usually it's the space where the merchandise stall is set up. On the left side, leading down the main standing area, is a long bar – nice and handy. Once in the standing area you can look back and up at the vast and elaborate smoke-stained ceiling. A painted proscenium arch perfectly draws your eye towards the stage. Importantly, there's plenty of space to get down the front. From virtually any position you get a clear unobstructed view of the stage… unless of course that tall fucker comes and stands directly in front of you.

Acoustically, it works a treat.

I've visited the T and C Club many times, off and on, over the years. My second time was in March 1988. I went to see Luxuria, supported by Xymox… a group of shoe-gazing bands on the eccentric 4AD label. Not the best gig ever, I have to say, although we were treated to an appearance by Morrissey reading some poetry. Other notables included the reunion of The Damned the same year, plus Cocteau Twins, Siouxsie and the Banshees, Killing Joke and – much later on – Groove Armada. All excellent gigs, some better than others. None has managed to reach the Top Ten, but the venue still holds a fascination for me. The weird thing is I can't put my finger on it. Maybe that's why I've never said, 'oh yeah, that's it! That's why I love seeing bands here.' There's no magical rhyme or reason, no science. It just works, and that'll do for me.

The magnificent Royal Albert Hall is probably one of the most beautiful venues in the world. It was built in 1871 for Queen Victoria and dedicated to her late husband. It's a splendid venue and well deserves its Grade I listing. Its circular design is an architectural masterpiece. Inside is like entering the first class lounge of the Orient Express. Everywhere is lush. There are two rows of small, quaint, private boxes. Above is a circle of seating. The gallery area, high in the gods, circles the whole venue. High above, hanging from the oval roof, are a series of white round discs designed to help with the acoustics.

Downstairs is a flat floor space, for seats or standing. The stage is a simple flat area dwarfed by the monstrous organ Matt Bellamy famously played during one of Muse's visits… The round design enables everyone to get a clear view of the stage. There are even seats in the choir area behind the stage. I remember getting tickets to see Paul Simon, together with the beautiful Ladysmith Black Mambazo, play his *Graceland* album. I sat in the choir area behind the open main stage, my jaw well and truly dropped. Paul waved to us, acknowledging our slightly off-centre view. It was such a special event. The *Graceland* album is wonderful and a graceful classic. Built on beautiful African rhythms, it naturally sways. The gig was nothing but magical, performed to perfection in a temple.

There's something very special about seeing a band here. It's a bit like an invasion. This palace was designed for orchestras, not rock bands. Once I asked what time the band would be on stage.

One of the ticket staff replied, 'our concerts normally start at 7:30.' Somehow it's a fabulous venue for rock and quality indie gigs. This theatre of concertos and oratorios becomes a cathedral for rock opera. It's that rare place where I'll buy seated tickets as I know I can stand up and not piss loads of people off. I know too that the sound will be great and I can spoil myself. Why not? I've been doing this gig thing for a long time and I deserve going first class once in a while.

I always look forward to seeing the line-up for the annual Teenage Cancer Trust series that Roger Daltrey helps organise and front. Over recent years the Trust has used the RAH to raise awareness of their cause – and get significant revenue too. Many major bands have offered their support. In 2008 I managed to get box tickets to see Muse headline. I'm always stunned by how much sound this band can make with so few instruments. They're simply the greatest rock band of this period – and boy, they give it out loud.

The beauty of the Albert Hall is that, while a temple to music, it also requires bands to strip back their shows to a more basic level. The stage isn't large enough for huge screens, massive banks of speakers, or scaffolding for millions of lights. All this stuff doesn't look right. Yes, bands can make a noise but it can be achieved with a pared-down stage set.

While holding some five and a half thousand people, the RAH also subtly transforms to a place of genuine intimacy. Its shape brings the audience closer to the band and each other. You feel part of your fellow musos' intensity and rapture. It's a great venue to take time to look at the crowd and see faces staring at the band, lost in concentration. There's a real sense of magic here.

While the majestic setting and clear acoustics stand out, the real difference is that bands really seem to love being there. You can feel the buzz. Just as top class footballers relish playing on a good surface, I feel that musicians also raise their game to match the privileges it offers. Bands famed for huge stage set and blasting sounds revel in the chance to refocus their show on the music rather than the art, videos and sets. Bands like The Who, Siouxsie, Muse, Depeche Mode and The Cure have all delivered awesome sets here. I love it. It's one place I always leave smiling, relaxed and well sorted. I can't wait to go back.

But.

Let's be honest. I bet you that, if given a choice or just one wish, you'd like to see your favourite close up. Nice and close. So close you can smell the band's hospitality rider on their breath. So close you can lean over and pluck the guitar or tap a note on the keyboard.

We all want to be there, be intimate, be in that band and on that stage.

To achieve this we must go local and small. I know that every decent-sized town and city has a range of small, low-key places where on some night in the week a band will climb on a tiny, cramped stage and for an hour or so perform their hearts out. These venues vary so much. They range from the dodgy health and safety trap to the newly decked back room of the local boozer. They're united in their simple and basic arrangements. The fixed lights, the hired set of speakers balancing on well-battered metal stands and the varying backdrop. The band usually have to walk through the crowd... usually full of their mates... and step up to the stage which is liberally cluttered with gear.

It's here, in these raw places, that you really feel music. You can't help it; in fact it's so intimate that you become part of the band. In front of you are life-sized people who are often very nervous, but doing something they really love. Of course we all love being there. Being right down the front.

It isn't fair to suggest a favourite venue on my journey, as there are simply far too many to see. I've visited a number of them as part of my journey. In fact I've set myself the task, when away, of seeking them out. Ezio have been a useful band in helping broaden my horizons. For example, they've taken me to The Cluny in Newcastle, a small pub on an industrial estate in Leeds and the famous Half Moon in Putney. The former is a well-established venue on the circuit, a place where students, folk people and local Geordie musos mix happily. The Leeds venue is that type of pub-with-a-stage venue where the landlord trades in cash, the regulars get a free gig and you're nervous about leaving as it's in the middle of an industrial estate with few streetlights and no public transport. I visited the Half Moon in Putney in the summer holidays of 1985 – partly because I just wanted to get the feel and soak up the atmosphere of this small, south London venue – here I saw a band called Terry and Jerry, who were a kind of contemporary rockabilly duet.

Some bands take you to some of the weirdest and most frightening places. Nic and I travelled one Easter holiday to see the excellent Oxford band Chatshow play in the Mitre pub just off the Blackwall Tunnel. Now, that was a venue. It was here that they held the Tunnel Club, where up-and-coming comedians got a real pasting. This pub is just off (i.e. a few feet away from) the southbound exit of the famous road tunnel. Hundreds of thousands of vehicles must go past every single day. If the landlord could set up a toll he'd be out of there in a week. Chatshow were a kind of Cult-Goth band. Great guitars supported by power chords and electronics. We loved them… so much we travelled to this them play mid-week in this bleak venue.

We arrived before the band. Looking around, we realised we were the only people there. After half an hour a few Goths arrived, trebling the crowd. Chatshow were next in, and entered into a dialogue with the landlord about playing. I wasn't sure who was most let down, but for thirty minutes our journey risked being a complete waste of time. Eventually a deal was struck, and Chatshow agreed to play.

Credit to them, they played a great gig. Nic and I bopped around with the other twenty nutters who had got there to see them. They played a quick encore and then it was off home. The band packed up quickly. Before heading west they had just enough time to raid the display cabinet of booze.

Cambridge, like any decent town and city, has its own range of small venues. I've visited most. Some, sadly, have gone. Many, amazingly, have survived. While they're not always putting on bands, every now and then they'll pull out the ace card. Graham Coxon played The Soul Tree in May 2009. In this small venue – more styled for disco nights than live music – it was, naturally enough, standing room only. He made it hard for most of the expectant crowd, though, by sitting on a small stool throughout his set and playing nothing from Blur.

Mitcham's Corner in Cambridge has an oversupply of small venues. It has two. There's a small room for about fifty people on the first floor of the Boat House pub. It's very intimate. I've seen Ezio and a local emerging band called Fred's House play great sets there. When it gets full it's the type of place you ask those at the front to move forward. The other is the Portland Arms, which has just had its back room completely revamped. I recently saw Robin Guthrie, the guitar bit of Cocteau Twins, play there recently, which was lush.

Now, these places attract a certain type of music. Yes, it would be great to see Muse, or The Cure or even the Stones play there but, let's be honest, their amps alone would fill the place. One note through volume 11 of the Marshall amp would knock the place down. No, these venues need bands that require contemplation, space to dream, that offer a chance to slip away blissfully into a musical bubble. Too often the gathering crowd are louder than the band. To me this is disrespectful. I find myself edging forward to distance myself from the gossipers, who – on that rare occasion, a night out together – sometimes turn out to include my wife…

Anyway… What's great about these venues, compared with all the paraphernalia of big gigs, is that you can really feel and enjoy the passion and energy of the performer. Every note is clearer. The banter is real. It just feels how music should be: you, them and everyone together. It doesn't matter who's playing. You never know where they will end up – and it doesn't matter. At the end of the show, after their first encore, it's too much hassle to leave the stage – so the crowd scream, and the band pick up their instruments and play. Then the house lights brighten and the crowd start talking again. The band then mingle with the audience and you compliment them on a great show. It sounds crass, but it is simply lovely. If you don't have one of these venues, create it. I know it will work and you never know who might turn up.

Now, I'm nervous about cover or tribute bands. Some are shocking and likely to get a real kicking if anyone turns up from the band they're copying. Some, though, have surprised me. The Australian Pink Floyd Show are exceptional and well worth a viewing. Close your eyes, forget you're where you are and you could actually be listening to the real McCoy.

Over the past few years a number of my Cambridge crew had been speaking highly of a local ska cover band. For various reasons, though, I had not been to see them. Then one winter evening they announced a fundraising event in the Black Bull pub in the neighbouring village. Ironically my old school friend Hugo was coming to Cambridge to celebrate his uncle's 80th birthday – I said he must stay with us. So no sooner had he arrived than we zoomed over to Longstanton and the Black Bull.

The Black Bull is not a regular music venue. It's a nice pub that has been warmly modernised and neatly extended at the back. There's just enough space to have a stage area for the band, with room for dancing immediately in front. Very intimate.

The pub was busy and had the air of a typical Saturday night at the local. Everyone seemed to know each other. Even though we were from only 'down the road,' we were outsiders. A number of us had made the short trip over, so we felt in good company... I was expecting it to kick off; you can never tell. Tony seemed to know a lot of the faces and we spent the first few pints being introduced to new folk. Some of the crowd were appropriately dressed. Fred Perry shirts… different colours… plenty of baldness… a couple of real skinheads… the old pair of real red Doc Martens, one pair with yellow laces. As I chatted away, a housing colleague brushed past.

'Hey Chris,' I said. 'How are you?'

'Hi Adam. I'm great, thanks. How's your work?' he asked. We spent a few minutes catching up on business and our local youth football teams. We were both involved with teams for the under-nines.

'Are you here to see the band?' he enquired.

'Yes. I've never seen them before. Lots of people have been talking about them. Good live, I hear. What about you? Have you seen them before?'

'Yes I have. In fact, I'm in the band. I play the trumpet,' Chris coolly let out.

'What? You're kidding!' I grinned with a mix of amusement and embarrassment. 'I'm sorry, I never knew. That's fantastic!'

I was quite taken aback. It turned out, as I watched the band walk across to the makeshift stage, that I also knew other members of this local band with a big reputation. When not in the band, Gary – with whom I was on good nodding and 'how are ya?' terms with – worked at the Junction. He was lead vocal. Then there was Dave on bass, who also ran the local youth football team but had previously played in our Sunday football league. I was happily shocked by the multitude of connections. Hugo could only smile.

The band, Big Ten, lived up to their reputation. They played an excellent set of well-orchestrated ska covers. All the classics: Madness, The Specials, The Selecter, The Beat… the odd couple of Dexy's tracks and a few older-school ska tunes. We had a ball.

Everyone knew the words and enjoyed reminiscing.

It was so good that Tony and I went to see Big Ten play another excellent set at the Black Bull a few months later. Whether it was knowing the band, an even larger Fred Perry-clad crowd, the extra pints or simply an even better play list, the second set took off. For an hour, thirty middle-aged bald men and dressed-up ladies danced the evening away. It was a gem. Big Ten covered their heroes and themselves in glory. I came away thinking what an excellent night I had just spent, jumping around to a brilliant set of unassuming local lads play some of the best songs from my youth in a small unpretentious venue a short bike ride from my front door. Bloody lovely.

Eleven: **I'm a Celebrity... Nice to Meet You**

I am puzzled as the newborn child
I am troubled at the tide:
Should I stand amid the breakers?
Should I lie with death my bride?
Hear me sing, 'Swim to me, swim to me,
     let me enfold you:
Here I am, here I am, waiting to hold you'

"Song to the Siren" by Tim Buckley and Larry Beckett

I EXPECT — WELL, IN FACT I KNOW — we all get a thrill from meeting someone famous. Someone who has been in the papers or written a brilliant song; somebody maybe we've creepily admired for decades from the solitude of our bedrooms. Such people, for us mere mortals, live on a different planet, surrounded by security and the odd groupie. It simply wouldn't be rock 'n' roll if these famous people didn't live lives we could only fantasise about. For some reason, lost in that time of a world without constant media, YouTube, Twitter and (many moons ago) TV, such people were called *stars*.

For various reasons in my wonderful gig-going years, I've been quite fortunate to actually meet a few stars, celebs and music icons. Now, I'm not a groupie, and though I love music and highly respect many musicians, I don't want to chase after them or stalk them in any way. Although they've been ordained to celebrity status and get photographed everywhere they go, they're still human — well, some of them — and they deserve, like you and me, some private space. They don't need a nerd like me chasing after them.

On the other hand, those of us who *aren't* celebs, stars or music icons are all intrigued by the status of those who *are*, and want to know more about their real side rather than the tabloid version we're sold daily. We also want to be able to say to friends that we've met such celebs, knowing that for a fleeting moment our pals will actually listen to our stories.

Meeting and – even worse – greeting a celebrity isn't easy. You hear stories about people meeting their idols and instantly losing the power of speech. Or spending hours in the venue loo, too ashamed to come out, having simply said, 'oh, I like your shirt,' to someone famous when in fact they should have said, 'what do you mean by the lyrics of the third track on your new album?' There's also the fear that your idol will simply look you in the eye and say, 'fuck off and leave me alone!'

One of my horror stories of this kind is when I was travelling back from Durham on the train and found myself in the same carriage as Roger – yes Roger Daltrey CBE. By the time this meeting took place I'd done a deal with myself. 'If I meet anyone famous, I'll approach them politely and introduce myself.' This was prompted by one of those horrid recurring nightmares that you're within touching distance of said celeb and you fall into the huge hole in the pavement designed by the Department of Missed Chances. One too many of a series of regretful encounters warranted this agreement I made with myself.

So here I was on a train. It was pretty empty so there weren't many people to annoy. Roger was sitting a few seats away. So I put down my stuff and got settled. After ten minutes I boldly walked along the carriage to where Roger and his companion were seated.

'Roger Daltrey?' I said, checking.

'Yes?' he slightly glared back.

'I don't want to interrupt you on your journey. I just wanted to say thank you for a brilliant gig the other day at the Albert Hall and for producing such great music.'

'Thanks,' he said, and smiled slightly – though clearly not wishing to enter into a deep and heavy.

We shook hands. I smiled. I shook hands with his travelling companion, who seemed slightly more interested and reasonable. I returned to my seat, proud that I had made my introduction but feeling pretty let down that we had not had an in-depth chat about The Who and engaged in some real storytelling. Maybe he was tired, I thought. Then again, I bet Pete Townsend would have been more approachable. Maybe I should have said 'Hi Roger. I'm a Gooner too. Nice to meet you.' I felt let down.

From my semi-radical political days at Oxford Poly I got very engrossed in the emerging housing crisis of the time. In the late 1980s, housing was becoming a real crisis… sadly it remains a major issue today. Homelessness had doubled and many more single people were ending up on the streets. The other side of Thatcher's housing policy was becoming painfully evident. My professional career saw me become ever more involved, and by the early 1990s I was working for a leading housing association. I was doing my bit in getting a range of affordable homes built. My specific interest in homelessness never dwindled, and doesn't to this day. In 1992 I was invited to join the national charity representing single homeless people, Crisis, and duly became a trustee a few years later.

The one thing I admire about celebrities is that many of them care passionately about a charity or issue and give considerable sums of money or time to their cause. David Gilmour from Pink Floyd, for example, has for many years been a supporter of Crisis. Why? I've no idea. Maybe it had something to with Syd Barrett's breakdown. David is a very private person, and it took everyone by surprise when he suddenly announced that he was selling his London property near Little Venice and giving the proceeds – the whole damn lot – to Crisis.

When I said that many celebrities give a *lot* of money to their cause, not many will ever give this kind of huge sum. At the time it was regarded as the largest single personal donation ever given to a UK charity. The donation was conditional on setting up an unusual housing project in London, replicating the work of the Common Ground housing project in New York. We called it the Urban Village project and it was to provide ex-homeless people the chance to live in secure accommodation alongside 'key workers'… important folk, such as nurses, teachers, firemen and social workers, who keep everything functioning. The New York version showed that people who had been homeless, now living in this way, had a greater chance of successfully re-engaging in society.

But to make it work we needed lots more cash. So Crisis embarked on a huge media campaign on a programme of meet-and-greet to attract other potential donors.

At this time Sir David Bell was our Chairman (and that of the *Financial Times*). A lovely, down-to-earth chap. Sir David offered to put on a buffet lunch in his palatial top-floor office in the Strand overlooking the Thames and most of London. The art deco surrounds, complete with brown leather chairs and works of art hanging from the cream walls, are exquisite – it was the perfect venue to wine, dine and wow donors. The luncheon guests ranged from the rich and famous to the very rich and extremely famous. All were supporters of Crisis and the sole purpose of this very smart lunch was to seek further large-scale donations for this housing idea. David Gilmour agreed to come along.

After a few speeches and votes of thanks, we started chatting and headed over to the buffet. I was hungry and so, apparently, was Mr Pink Floyd. I genuinely didn't see him make his move, which perfectly matched mine. We met over the pile of white plates next to the extraordinary Michelin-star buffet. A gastronomic feast of spicy prawns, asparagus wraps, stilton puff pastry parcels. Now, I'm pretty good at professional chin-wagging. I've always coped well with talking to high profile people, politicians and key decision-makers.

But here I was standing, craning over a range of succulent buffet snacks, next to the man who wrote *Dark Side of the Moon*, *Wish You Were Here* and the most amazing track off *The Wall*, "Comfortably Numb." I know friends who would have poisoned me to be here. I was here and they weren't. But what on earth do you say to this musical God?

'Would you like a sandwich?' was too basic. 'What's "Wish You Were Here" about?' too deep.

I looked up from the table and simply turned to David, introduced myself and said, 'thank you very much for such a generous donation.' I was a trustee and he was the donor. It was right and proper.

He turned to me. The slight pause made me think, 'shit. I've blown it.'

'Thank you,' he said. 'I appreciate your thanks. What do you do?' he asked.

'I work for a housing association near Cambridge. I help get the new affordable homes built,' I replied, all the while thinking, 'bloody hell, this is surreal, or have I missed the plot?'

For a few more minutes we talked about housing and a bit about Cambridge. The smell of the glorious food was now too much and we tucked in. We smiled and departed. We never said one word about music, and I'm calmly pleased we didn't because I probably couldn't have handled it.

A few years later Shaks Ghosh, the Chief Executive of Crisis at the time, told me her story about when David Gilmour actually confirmed his donation and the precise amount. It's a story I'll never forget, so please forgive the digression.

A meeting was planned in a posh London hotel. The donation was now widely known about but, bizarrely for Crisis, it hadn't been formalised. There wasn't a letter or even a cheque. The meeting was set up to get it confirmed.

Shaks was advised to dress smartly and to be feminine, not her normal style. One of the Crisis customers agreed to join her. He went and hired a full dinner jacket, black tie job. They waited in the palatial bedroom suite. There's a knock on the door. Standing in front of them is David. He's wearing jeans and a dirty food-stained T-shirt – rock 'n' roll, man. For an hour and half they chatted away. Then David announced that his chauffeur was waiting and it was time to go. However, while the project and donation were mentioned briefly, the precise deal and all its important formalities were still not confirmed. Shaks felt dejected. As they stood outside the hotel on the London pavement a scruffy man shambled up to them. 'Excuse me, guv. Can you spare any change, ta?'

We get this dilemma in the housing world regularly. Do you give money to people who beg? The hard line is that you don't – sadly, many people who beg will simply blow it on drink, drugs or whatever their vice is. A quick fix but not the long-term solution.

David, though, pulled out his wallet and passed over a crisp fifty quid note. The man's eyes popped out like a puppet. He clasped on to it hard. Shaks took in a deep gasp.

'Thank you. Thank you,' the man repeated and sped off. His eyes bulging.

'That was incredibly generous of you, David,' said Shaks, still in shock.

'Generous? Hardly. I've just given you three and a half million quid.' With that, Shaks hugged the man who had just confirmed the largest single private donation ever given to a charity at that time. Then they waved good-bye. Job done.

I have my link and bond with Crisis to this day. It's a unique organisation and attracts an eclectic mix of supporters. Another avid supporter of Crisis was and is Paul Weller, the Modfather. As leader and founder member of The Jam – surely one of the most important and influential bands of the late 1970 and 1980s – he probably created as many musos then as there are people with a mobile phone today. I was really lucky to have seen them play a few times at small venues in London. In these smaller places the crowd of jubilant but rebellious youth – all cramped together – could reach out and literally touch them. You felt you were part of the story. The Jam caught the mood of a generation of kids who had suffered enough and needed a way to express their anger.

In the late 1990s, Crisis started to arrange a few charity events as a way of connecting with younger audiences while generating important donation income. The charity had been going for thirty years and was now growing fast. To celebrate, it was decided to put on a special gig titled 'Under the Heavens' on Sunday, 29 March 1998, at the recently built reconstruction of Shakespeare's Globe Theatre on the South Bank, London. Paul Weller, by now immensely famous and a national hero with a compelling solo career, was asked to join the celebrations. He agreed to play, but on the condition that the gig was not publicly promoted using his name. He would be known and referred to as 'Very Special Guest.' But I knew.

I told Ken and Stu. I also let my Weller-mad friend Rachael into secret. It was only fair.

'Are you sure he'll be playing?' they all said separately. 'Look I'm on the Board, it's confirmed. We simply can't go public on it. Trust me.'

We made our way to London and all met up outside the beautifully restored Globe Theatre. The white timber-framed structure looks completely out of place and time, but it's lovely. Small and very compact. The downstairs area is all-standing and exposed to the elements. The boxes in the upper rows have wooden benches covered by a perfect thatch roof to keep the rich dry.

The Under the Heavens event was supported by Beth Orton, Rory Bremner and the Cardboard Citizens. It was an evening of poetry, dance, comedy and music. Everyone gave great performances. A few celebs gave speeches saying that all we wanted to do was to stop homelessness. Although nobody said, I expect everyone knew who the Very Special Guest was. It had become the worst-kept secret in town.

At 9.00 pm the compere, Ardal O'Hanlon, came to stage front and gave a huge 'thank you' to everyone for coming and supporting Crisis. Ardal, like so many, talked about the continuing scandal of the homelessness problem in the country – food for thought.

Then – 'I'm now proud to introduce tonight's Very Special Guest. Ladies and gentlemen, please welcome on stage… *Mr Paul Weller!*'

The place went mad. By now we were down the front. If the Globe had a roof it would by now be floating off under Tower Bridge. Guitar in hand, Weller went straight in. Fantastic. I looked around. Ken had this massive grin and was bouncing around like a kangaroo, Paul was smiling and Rachael was crawling around the sawdust-covered floor looking for her torn-out eyes.

After the show I pulled out the ace card. As a trustee for Crisis I was invited to attend a special post-event party. I gathered our group for some excited banter about such a brilliant performance by Weller but also such a wonderful show altogether. All part of the post-gig ritual. Suddenly everyone becomes the music critic. Tonight we all agreed this show scored five stars.

'Anyone fancy a drink?' I asked.

'Where can we get one now? Everywhere's closed,' Ken sensibly replied. He was right, of course. Those were the days before open-all-hours drinking times.

'I know where.' I paused theatrically. Then, nonchalantly: 'I can take you all to the post-gig party…'

'What?' they all said in perfect unison.

'I've got an invitation to the post-party event. I'm on the guest list and you're my guests,' I lifted my arms up wide into the air, like a Shakespearean actor.

Everyone's eyes bulged open and their eyebrows went into a merry spin. They were speechless.

'Come on then,' I commanded. With that the posse broadened their already overstretched grins and we marched up to the side door with a handwritten VIP sign on it. I introduced myself to the Crisis staff member on the door and politely indicated my guests to her.

'That's fine,' she said, and in we walked. It was a large events room directly underneath the Globe. The understage area was a bit like entering a theatrical tardis. It was huge. A vast area, plainly decorated – in any other arena it would have been a car park. A mixed crowd of people were gathering. We picked up a beer from the hospitality table. This strange collection of folk from all walks of life, ages and cultures made it feel a bit like a wedding after the speeches. Everyone seemed happy. They should have been; they had just seen a great gig and it was now time to mingle.

Our little group stood there, bottle of beer in hand, looking around the range of faces and attires. This was my first venture backstage after a gig and, frankly, I didn't know what went on or (more importantly) what to do. I remember reading years ago about the hedonistic Depeche Mode after-show gigs where anything apparently seemed to go on. I couldn't quite see the Globe or my charity entertaining that. It remained a private dream.

It was then that I noticed a table with a slightly larger gathering than others. It seemed a proper family affair, with kids, mums, dads and grandparents. One of the crowd then headed over our way. I thought that face was familiar. He walked past, smiled, headed off to get a few beers and then briskly walked back. Everyone in the now pretty packed place seemed pleased to see him.

It was Paul himself. Yes, the Modfather had just walked past us and smiled. He, that very man, that musician, that singer, that lead performer, that God. He was here amongst us.

Our posse seemed to dissolve. How do you handle a situation where you were within touching distance of a living icon? Well, as a muso growing in confidence there was only one thing I could do. You would go up to said icon, introduce yourself, saying something reasonably coherent, walk away, smile and then report the incident to friends and family whenever the chance arose.

Now, this may seem easy. To many this is an everyday occurrence. But icons are *icons*. In muso terms, an icon holds a higher position than any spirit or even God. As a reasonably rational person I had played this through many times but then, like a brilliant track or a classic version of your favourite song ever, the eco light bulb in my head slowly lit up. This is in fact *my* gig. This is *my* charity. I'm a trustee. The event was a celebration of our 30 years' struggle to remedy one of the failures of 'civilised' society: appalling homelessness. Paul, though an icon, was our guest. He was here supporting Crisis and our work.

Without any apology, I left our crowd standing on the spot with their bottles and polite silence. I walked over to Paul, who by now had returned to his family and his posse. Without hesitation I went up to the man who made men cry, who gave generations hope, who gave so many of my friends a reason to believe, a reason even to live.

'Hello Paul,' I said slightly formally. 'Can I introduce myself? I'm Adam Broadway, I'm a trustee of Crisis. I just wanted to thank you for playing for us tonight. It was a brilliant show'.

Now, in most normal situations I'd expect the icon to smile, maybe shake my hand and without speaking show me the door. But no.

Paul listened and grabbed my hand and said, 'it was a pleasure, mate. Absolute pleasure. I'm really pleased you liked the set. I'm delighted to support your work. Terrific.'

For the next five minutes we engaged in an open conversation about housing, music and homelessness. It was a normal chat, just like you and I would have if we were to meet.

I was conscious of this privileged position and saw my chance to leave, though I wasn't looking for one, without being rude. We shook hands and I left. I walked upright, like a king to my troops. Throughout all this they had watched from close by.

'Fucking hell, Ad,' Ken said. 'That was Paul Weller. What did he say?'

I told them about our conversation. For me it had been simple and direct. But for most people this was a scene only played out in a dream.

Rachael listened intently. I sensed her admiration was dampened by jealousy. At this moment Paul walked past again to collect a few beers from the drinks table. On his return I saw my second chance.

'Paul? Sorry to bother you. Can I introduce my friend Rachael? She's a massive fan.'

'Hi Rachael,' he said genuinely. Rachael blushed and they shook hands. There were no other words said.

'Thanks,' I said to Paul. He returned to his family. I looked at Rachael – her eyes were full of tears and absolutely nothing audible could crawl out of her gaping jaw.

'I told you he would be here,' I said. With the drama over and mission successfully completed, we went home. I don't think anyone said another word all night. There was nothing to say. It was time to reflect and soak it all up.

Not all things go or come that easily. I introduced myself to Jarvis Cocker once. We were at Latitude Festival in 2009, our first trip. The great attraction of Latitude was the range and variety of events, from music to poetry, opera to comedy. It was also a small festival, easily navigable, set in a wonderful wooded park around a mill pond lake. The event attracted a wide range of folk. A number of celebrities openly mooched about.

On of these walkabout between the stages, Jenny spotted, Jarvis Cocker. He did rather stand out, wearing a green tweed jacket, bright cords and long black boots.

I'm not alone in this slightly strange world. I'm not a crank or a stalker – life is too busy and interesting for that. On the other hand, musical stars, idols and geniuses have often done something that has had such an important influence on my enjoyment of this short time on earth. When the chance arises, therefore, I just want to say 'thank you' to them.

I'm not the only one. At this precise moment in any bar, pub, restaurant or club from Brighton to Glasgow, I bet there's someone recounting how they bumped into a famous local star or celebrity in their local supermarket. I'm sure that right now there's someone showing off a selfie of them with their arm round a now shy, slightly scarred-for-life star next to the fruit aisle in Sainsbury's.

Having the balls to approach and engage with a celeb needs confidence and the all-important ability to take the shrug-off, 'yeah, get lost' – or indeed the harder, 'fuck off you twat,' version some stars think their fame and fortune allows them to dispense.

Nic used this to great reward in Switzerland when he turned up on spec at an Ozzy Osbourne gig in Lausanne only to find that it was completely sold out. Now, being the cheeky chappie that he is, Nic headed straight for the stage door and waited patiently for Ozzy, Sharon and their entourage to arrive. Banking on the fact that his English voice would stand out from the Swiss/French/Italian crowd, Nic called out to Ozzy that he had come all the way from England for the gig only to find it sold out, and was there any way that they could get him in. 'We'll see what we can do,' was Ozzy's reply, which could easily have been code for, 'fuck off you dick.' But sure enough, Sharon came back out 20 minutes later, pointed at Nic, and told the security guard that he was with her. Nic jumped over the security barriers and Sharon took him to watch the gig with her from side stage!

To this day Nic can't quite believe what happened to him and says he spent the whole gig expecting to wake up out of some crazy dream. But it was for real. Big respect to Ozzy and Sharon for treating a fan that way.

Now, Stu tells a great story of meeting Dee Dee Ramone. For Stu this was his ticket to paradise. The Ramones were and remain his favourite band, though sadly many of them have gone to guitar heaven. The 'When Stuey Met Dee Dee' story goes something like this.

> The first time I met Dee Dee Ramone was at the Hammersmith Palais in 1981. I'd bunked off school on the day of the gig and was aiming to get up there early to try and find a way of getting in to see my heroes, the Ramones, do their soundcheck. I can't remember now where this idea had come from, but I've got a feeling that at some earlier gig I'd heard them warming up with my ear pressed up against an outside door or something. This time I wanted to go one better.
>
> As I arrived at the Palais, the main doors to the venue were open. I don't suppose they were expecting many punters to be arriving at 9.00 am. I crept in and hid behind some conveniently stacked chairs at the back. It was perfect. I could see the stage and, as long as no one came to move the chairs, I'd never be seen.
>
> Of course I was seen. After several hours crouched behind a stack of chairs, a member of the Palais staff ambled over and asked me if I wouldn't mind leaving as the band had arrived. I was gutted. There was still Plan B, though: I'll ask the band if I can stay.
>
> As I walked back out on to the Shepherd's Bush Road I

saw Dee Dee getting off the tour bus. I ran up to him and asked if I could come in with the band. 'Yeah, sure,' was the reply. As I happily strolled in, however, the jobsworth that had asked me to leave ten minutes earlier spotted me in the entourage. When challenged, Dee Dee said, 'hey, I'm Dee Dee Ramone. This is a friend of mine,' but jobsworth wasn't having any of it. Out I went for a second time.

Within a couple of minutes, however, there was Dee Dee appearing from a side door. He called me over and I was in! We sat and chatted while the stage was being set up. We talked about various things and he seemed genuinely interested in other bands I'd seen, the venues I'd been to and, in particular, where I thought the Ramones should play in London.

I said, 'The Lyceum is a great venue.' And sure enough, the next time they played London they played four nights there – anything to do with me?

We chatted a bit about Motorhead as I'd seen them a few times and it turned out he was good mates with Lemmy. He was just the nicest, friendliest bloke you could ever wish to meet.

I've absolutely no idea now what tracks they played or how long they played for. I stayed with them throughout the evening. As Dee Dee was leaving he asked me if I needed any tickets as he had some spare for the next evening.

The Ramones had added an extra midnight gig at The Venue in Victoria. Nic and I had tickets for the downstairs standing, but our mate, who was coming to his first Ramones gig, could only get a ticket for the upstairs seats. I was sure that Dee Dee could sort Steve out with a ticket for downstairs with us.

Finding the stage door for The Venue was proving a bit of an obstacle as we wandered around the back streets and alleyways of Victoria in the dark. But luckily we caught sight of the tour bus and chased after it for just long enough to see where the band were making their way in.

I knocked on the door, introduced myself as a friend of Dee Dee Ramone's and asked if it would be ok to speak to him. A few minutes later, the stage door opened again and there was Dee Dee! I explained the ticket situation and he said to go back round to the front and he'd get us put on the guest list: Stuart plus five (we'd picked up a couple of ticketless stragglers on the way).

It was getting later and later and 'Stuart plus five' was not looking good for finding its way on to the guest list. So back round to the stage door. Another few minutes went by and there was Dee Dee again. He thought about it for a second or two (it did look as if thinking was getting considerably more difficult by this stage) and told us all to come in! In we went and followed him along some corridors, down some stairs and into the Ramones' dressing room. He told us to sit and wait for a few minutes while the band finished an interview. It was all hustle and bustle with various crew and management running around, people scribbling notes and others taking pictures. And there, sat in the corner on a wooden bench, was our little band of chancers!

We then followed Dee Dee through more corridors, down a spiral staircase and on to the stage where we all jumped into the crowd.

I got my chance to thank him again for this unbelievable opportunity several years later.

I was staying in New York for a week in 1993 with my girlfriend. She had absolutely no interest in music but granted me one day to trawl the record shops to see if I could find anything rare or unusual by the Ramones. There had to be something in New York!

It had been a pretty fruitless day but, finally, I got what seemed to be a really good lead. There was a record shop 'up the road a bit and round the corner' that sold bootlegs and was bound to have something by the Ramones. It was somewhere between Greenwich Village and the Chelsea Hotel. We entered the little record shop, and there, standing at the counter in mid-purchase of an X-Ray Spex bootleg cassette was Dee Dee Ramone! The man himself. What were the chances of that?

Now on best mate terms, I collared him as he left the shop. Dee Dee was the same friendly and engaging bloke I had met all those years before. He would have talked for hours. He couldn't remember our previous encounters (no surprise there!) but loved hearing about the other times I'd got to meet him. By now he had left the Ramones but was still writing songs for them so knew what they were all up to. He told us about what he'd been doing since he'd left and about the new band he'd put together. I had a couple of photos taken with him and then I let him get back to the Chelsea Hotel to listen to his X-Ray Spex tape!

Wot a story, I say.

Anyway, I digress from Jarvis at Latitude. Having been tipped off, I start to look at for the lead singer of Pulp. For many years Pulp were a simple indie rock outfit, waiting for their time and space to take the main stage. That time came when they produced and delivered one of best ever Britpop songs, "Common People." I loved it. Almost overnight this hard-working band achieved their desire. Jarvis – with his eccentric style, huge black rimmed specs and beanpole figure – was suddenly the lust kid of a generation.

I spotted him walking briskly past the food and drinks stall. Ben and I ambled towards the lake and then headed up to the main area. By now Jarvis was heading directly towards us. I noticed him, like a lion chooses its gazelle. I moved us slightly into his line of trajectory.

'Jarvis? Hi, I'm Adam,' I introduced myself politely, calmly, in a very matter-of-fact way.

Jarvis smiles broadly and greets me as if we're good or even long-lost friends. We didn't hug in that man bonding way. But it was a strong firm handshake.

But now what? Here we are, clenched hands, looking at each other.

'Just wanted to say 'hello' and say thanks for producing such great records,' I said genuinely.

Jarvis by this point suddenly realised that I wasn't some swanky film producer, some obscure record label owner, an adoring school friend or even a quality session guitarist. I was just a normal punter. A twat who liked music who had bought a few of his (or rather Pulp's) singles. I was a nothing. A no one. A paying visitor who didn't even have a VIP wristband.

Jarvis's smile disappeared as quickly as Pulp became a pop music hit.

To be fair he was polite. He thanked me and let go of my hand. He walked off. So did I. We went in exactly the opposite direction. Ben, during this momentous meeting, had carefully backed off just in case it had kicked off. Just in case Jarvis had turned into some judo nutter and threw me over his lightweight structure and hurled me into the comedy tent.

'That was Jarvis Cocker from a band called Pulp,' I informed my teenager. He bowed his head as teenagers seem to do. He didn't seem to share my enthusiasm, and neither did Jarvis.

Now, these brief meetings with muso celebs might have been… er, brief, and in many cases not very rewarding. But for me they've kind of added a bit of spice to this incredible journey. At times like these I've had that one-off chance, a 'one-on-one-with-the-keeper' moment, to get a personal brownie point. I've had a chance to say – face to face – *thank you*. Thank you for creating something that for years has been the fuel for my journey. Thank you for producing music, theatre and shows that, for so many interconnected reasons, have made me smile or cry. They've helped me to explode, or let off steam; most importantly they've offered some sense to this crazy world and given me hope to get through to tomorrow.

How many times have you regretted not giving a loved one a hug when they needed it, not crying when you're feeling emotionally broke, or ducking out of saying well-chosen and caring words to an ill relative, or not saying 'I love you' to someone close? Where I have genuine respect I intend to show it. Yes, my hard-earned money has in some part gone to giving my idols a life in dreamtime compared to mine, but for me they've given me something money would never have bought. And for that reason I'll continue to say *thank you*.

Twelve: **Top Gigs**

When you're sure you've had enough
Of this life
Well, hang on
Don't let yourself go
Everybody cries
And everybody hurts
Sometimes

"Everybody Hurts" by REM

LISTS. WHAT IS IT ABOUT CREATING A LIST? Is it our way of creating order? Many of us can't resist a list. Not shopping ones, though. I enjoy shopping, especially a trip to Ted Baker, which is so much more enjoyable than spending hours trying to get sense out of a salesperson in Sports Direct. We seem to be fixated with creating a list for virtually everything else.

I saw a list from the National Trust recently suggesting the Top Fifty things a kid should do before they're 11¾. And there's always some TV show listing the Top Ten weirdest stunts, haircuts, dangerous animals, potent drinks or, of course, the best hits from a musical decade. In music we seem obsessed with The Charts. Is it a British thing? Nick Hornby writes about it in his wonderful book *High Fidelity*. We seem to be better than other countries at creating a chart or league of Top Ten for anything sporting or musical.

I put it down to the *Top of the Pops* generation. For years, on a Thursday evening, every child across the land would put down their homework, reading book or (if late) knife and fork, and sit glued to the telly in rapt anticipation of the unveiling of the best-selling singles of the week. It was the programme you could not miss. For a would-be muso it was like attending church. If you missed it you'd be in confessional the very next morning. Even worse, if you didn't watch it and analyse each artist and their performance, and didn't know the Top Ten off by heart, you lost the bragging rights in the playground the next day.

Top of the Pops is etched in the minds of my generation. The video of Queen's "Bohemian Rhapsody," The Stranglers miming, Slade screaming "Merry Christmas," the appalling football songs, Bowie, Bolan and Blondie. My dad used to utter his displeasure but interestingly went very quiet when goggling at Suzi Quatro in her black leather trousers.

Top of the Pops created a new way of summing the world up. Everything as a chart. The 'A' list. Top Ten Ever Dance Tracks. Top Fifty Guitar Riffs. Top Ten Goals scored by a defender. Our own Top Ten songs.

Over my gig-going years I've seen something close to 700 gigs. Not just bands but actual gigs. Festivals have to be classified differently, in my opinion. They can only count as *one* gig. It's easy to see thirty to fifty bands in one good festival. I'm talking about *actual gigs*. This equates to some thousand-odd bands. Along the way I've collected a mental record of my Top Ten gigs. But I have a huge problem. When I actually sit down and list my Top Ten I find I have over fifty contenders. So how could I choose a Top Ten? Having spent a third of a century gigging, what could I seriously consider as a Top Ten gig?

There are many attributes that go to make a gig memorable; and there are others that make it *special*. But even in the mayhem of so much variety, numbers and an ageing memory, some gigs (for various reasons) simply stand out and proud from the crowd. Well, Pop Pickers, here's a few of my Top Gigs.

The first gig I want to put on my list is Genesis at the wonderful Hammy Odeon. By the time I got to see Genesis they were massive. They had become the prog rock world champions but they had also lost one of their inspirations, Peter Gabriel. By then some genius Genesis albums had already provided the foundation for my record collection. In the late 1970s the beautiful gatefold sleeve album sleeves of *And Then There Were Three* and *A Trick of the Tale* were rarely filed away on the record shelf but left next to my record deck ready for another airing.

By 1982 I had fallen in love with music and a dream of a girlfriend. I had started my application to become a Hammy Odeon season ticket holder. So I was over the moon when I received the prepaid and self-addressed envelope containing the tickets to see Genesis at the Hammy. Of course as a muso with L plates I hadn't learnt the importance of controlling emotions prior to a gig. I would learn this later. At this one, though, I was so excited I can't recall how we got there. It was all a haze. I only came out of the dream and into the noise of west London when we turned the corner, walked under the Hammy flyover and saw, in bright red lights above the entrance, the word *Genesis*.

That evening Genesis played a truly remarkable and, more importantly, influential set. As the years fade I lose the detail, although I do know this gig had a profound effect on me. Genesis not only created the emotion I longed for, but also a visual experience that took me out of my mind and into their imaginary world. The light show was stunning. It was probably nothing special when compared with all the wizardry and pyrotechnics we see today. But back then, the range and variety of the changing set colours – so in tune with their grandiose music – was mind blowing. This was more than a show, it was an *experience*. I had never realised it was what I had wanted; now I was there, watching it *live*.

I smiled all the way home and don't recall saying much. My tiny mind was carefully collecting as much info as it could and storing it away. In one evening Genesis had raised the bar with a display of orchestral brilliance. Their complex and detailed compositions were journeys in their own right. Tonight these musical novels had been given a light and sound show of pure brilliance. My lord, everyone who followed would have to perform extremely well to get into my Top Gigs list.

Being a student wasn't about double maths or going to the student Monday night bike club disco, even though Nic was the DJ. It simply meant I could get to as many gigs as I wanted. Oxford Poly had two venues. The main hall, which catered for some thousand or so people, was more of a large show hall. A large box of a building. High ceiling, wooden floor, which in the summer season became that hated chamber where we would sit in silence with a pen in hand trying to steady the nerves doing our finals. For the rest of the year, especially at the weekend, it became our main venue for live music.

The other venue was the student bar. The SU bar, as it was better known. During the day it served lunches but at night it became a venue. It was the space for the numerous club discos and more intermittent gigs. In front of the servery at the opposite end from the bar we created a small stage area with some rather un-sturdy black folding platforms. Nic and I spent far too many nights here. Over our four-year courses it was here that we held our famous and hugely notorious pop quizzes. But that's another story.

In terms of gigs a few bands played in the SU bar, including The Chevalier Brothers, The Blow Monkeys, Pendragon and local bands such as the excellent Chatshow.

But one gig stood out. In 1984 The Pogues played there. The Pogues are probably mostly remembered for Shane MacGowan and his alcoholism, lack of teeth and that wonderful Christmas duet with the late Kirsty MacColl. The Pogues were a rough but simple Irish band who played Irish ballads at full throttle while slammed, to an equally slammed audience.

The gig was announced late but sold out immediately. Luckily a tip off from the Ents crew got me a couple of tickets. I eagerly awaited this Friday evening funfest. Their album *Rum, Sodomy and the Lash* summoned up a load of beerheads for a night of heavy boozing, heavy dancing and having a real *craic*.

The good news for the Ents crew was that The Pogues in their early years didn't have much gear. In typical Irish ceilidh style the band only needed a couple of mics, a guitar, a fiddle and a snare drum. The good news for the crowd was that this simple three-piece format would create a vibrant sound full of heart and rhythm. To this day I don't know why at our gig there were only three members of the band when in fact there were normally at least five. Anyway…

Shane was joined by the wonderful Cait O'Riordan and, I believe, Andy Ranken on snare drum. There was no hanging around – almost before they emerged from the Ents office-cum-backstage changing room, the buzzing crowd was jigging around.

I watched the gig from the side of the stage. It was mad down the front. For once I wanted to take in the whole show. I clung onto the small side wall while balancing on a chair. I happened to be recovering from a broken leg. My view was brilliant, touching distance, perfect for this small setting. Everything came together. The vibe from the band, their simple stories of difficult but real lives, mixed with a frenetic guitar and violin. It summed up why I love small pumping gigs. Everyone – especially Shane, Cait and Andy – were having an absolute ball. From my vantage point I could see all the detail. The wry smiles, the laughs, the one, two, three, fours. I was so close I felt part of the gig.

At the end of the evening, the crowd quickly dispersed. Noticing it was still open, I headed off to the bar at the end of the room. As I placed my order Cait jumped down from the stage, ran up to the bar and, with one arm on the counter, turned back to the stage. 'Hey Shane!' she screamed in her heavy Irish drawl.

'What the fuck d'ya want?'

'The bar's still open.'

Shane jumped down from the stage and ran over at full speed, only stopping at the bar because his small frame couldn't jump over it. There I was with a pint in my hand, standing next to the artists from one of the best gigs I would ever see. I was speechless. Cait and Shane downed the beers as if it were their first for months. In reality it was probably only an hour and a half since their last one.

Within a few weeks of the gig their album *Rum, Sodomy and The Lash* was in the charts and everyone was talking about them. The Pogues were now famous and the new fad. Irish folk music was now hip and trendy. Their show in our small tight venue summed up the thrill of seeing a band in such intimacy just before they became famous. Friends even today can't believe they missed the SU bar gig. I smile, knowing that I was there.

I'm pleased that I've developed a really eclectic taste in music. Of course there's some music I don't like or simply don't get, such as country and western, plenty of rap (some I get) and most industrial metal. On the other hand, coming from a rock and indie background the one modern music I adore is what I call dance. Dance cum trance. I think back to when Donna Summer released "I feel Love" way back in 1977. This pulsating track was one of my major musical influences. It has to be *the* track before its time. A decade in advance. I ended up buying two copies of it – I wore out the first. I was clearly programmed to enjoy dance music.

There are plenty of brilliant dance DJs out there. Everyone from Pete Tong and Tiësto to Armin Van Buuren and Oakenfold. New

DJs emerge all the time, but one guy that caught my interest early in his phenomenally rapid rise to fame was a guy from Canada, Joel Thomas Zimmerman, better known as Deadmau5. In 2009 Deadmau5 announced a gig at the Junction in Cambridge. I jumped at the chance to see the emerging legend – even if I would be one of the oldest in the crowd. Who cared? This was no reason not to go and see if this highly rated DJ could become the next sensation behind the decks.

I can't remember where I heard him the first time. I rarely found time for the radio, but certainly when I heard his first major single it ignited that 'I like that' gene in my body.

Some folk don't like dance music. Thatcher even tried to ban it. The thing that draws me to dance music is the subtle way the belting beats and rhythms pick you up and take you on a meandering rollercoaster. Up and down valleys, over hills, whisking you away, carefree. I prefer the more trance-type music I first heard at Glastonbury in the days before the huge dance tents were put up. The days of bands like Banco de Gaia and The Sabres of Paradise. Deadmau5, though, was new. Less trance-like, much heavier in tone and with a solid beat. All played between 110 and 140 bpm. Pumping. But I liked it. It resonated with me and I wanted to see if it worked well live.

The average age of the hands-in-the-air crowd was about eighteen until I strolled in. As there was only me and there were loads of them, it only rose by one base point. But I was the only 'oldie' in the place. It didn't and never does bother me. As I near my first half century and look forward to taking on the next, I'm oblivious to the backchat, the, 'oh, aren't you too old for going to concerts?' and the, 'aren't they young enough to be your kids?' hilarious comments.

Do you know what? I don't give a shit. I feel honoured to have reached this point in my journey. Having got this far I'll continue to strive for that perfect gig, the best set ever, the show that gets me saying, 'that's it, I've now seen everything.' I hope many of those I meet follow the same path.

The Deadmau5 gig was even better than expected. It was ear-piercingly loud and hard. It pumped out one of heaviest basses ever. On each side of Deadmau5's deck console there were vertical brilliant LED strip-lights; the man himself, appearing through clouds of dry ice, was kitted out in a large Mickey Mouse-type headpiece. It must have been suffocating in there. Huge respect to his fitness. For nearly two hours the Junction became a sound system heaven. The walls were mushed with bass, bright strobes and youthful sweat. Heads nodded, hands raised and fell in time; yelps and catcalls greeted the stand-out tracks. It wasn't long before my feet were moving and my hands itched to reach the black ceiling.

Tonight was a very special evening. Here I was, watching a new generation of musos listening to a future DJ giant. His sound was awesome. I'm not sure my Junction had ever been so badly beaten up by the bass before. In one small venue I had experienced a full-on DJ set. I came out buzzing.

Arguably it's the sound and how the band performs on the night that really match the judging criteria for what makes a Top Ten slot. But they're not the whole story. The wider gig experience is crucial. Like when we saw U2 at the RDS Arena in their home city of Dublin. It's definitely true that bands seem to perform best in front of home crowds. I don't know why.

The 1990s were a period of change. My riotous and debauched years of college life had passed. Jen and I were settling into our lives as respectable adults in the real world. Our desire for travel meant taking any chances we could for long weekends away. We'd heard good reports about Dublin and thought we'd give it a go, so we booked a short break for August 1993. U2 were now a world rock band but we'd both been privileged to see them play in small venues at the start of their epic journey in the early 1980s. I'd seen them at the Hammy Palais in 1982, Jen at the Bracknell Sports Hall earlier the same year.

It just so happened that our long weekend coincided with the band's homecoming from a massive world tour (The Zoo tour). We didn't have tickets and genuinely… well, kind of… weren't planning to go and see them. Dublin, however, was full of excitement that their boys were back in town. The whole city couldn't hide its enthusiasm.

After a day of shopping I thought, 'why not?'

'Shall we go to the gig?' I timed my proposal carefully. Jen was aware of the gig. While not a priority for her, I expected she was up for it.

'We don't have tickets,' she replied, with that female attention to detail.

'Yep, I know, but it's a large venue and there's a good chance someone will be selling,' I suggested.

'Ok, nothing really to lose,' I was slightly astonished about the reply. Then I smiled.

Off we set. The RDS stadium is a short journey out of the city, past the Lansdowne Road. We soon found ourselves walking along with a growing, eager crowd towards the stadium. We agreed to look out for people hanging around in the chance they might have a spare ticket. As we walked on I asked a few people if they had any spares. The first few just shook their heads. Then one bloke gave me that look that said, 'are you mad? Look! It's U2 in Dublin. Get real.'

I'm the ever-persistent type. I continued looking at the faces just in case. Suddenly a young man appeared a couple of feet in front of me. He seemed in a bit of a rush.

I don't know why but I called out, 'hey mate! You don't know of any spare tickets, do you?'

'How many d'ya want?' came the totally unexpected reply in a rich Irish accent.

'Two. It's for us.' I pointed to Jen and me, as if he needed any assurances.

'Yeah, I got two. Me mate and his girlfriend have just split up and they aren't going. You can have them.'

I was speechless. I then started to worry about the haggling over the extortionate prices which was bound to follow.

'How much do you want for them?' I asked, preparing for the worst. Jen and I hadn't agreed a top price. Of course now that we were here that price would get even higher.

'Face value, mate. It's dem that lost out,' he casually replied.

The heavens had opened. Above me was a rather overweight figure with a long white beard. He was smiling.

I had heard of the phrase 'the luck of the Irish' but never the luck of an Englishman in Dublin asking for two U2 tickets. We quickly exchanged the cash for two lovely pristine gig tickets. There was a large bar a few feet away. It was loud and heaving. My now best-ever mate said he was going to get a drink.

'Come on mate, I'll get you one.' I grabbed his arm and shoved a pint of the black stuff in his hand. He smiled, raised his glass and disappeared.

Jen and I downed a beautiful pint of Guinness… it does taste better in Dublin… and headed into the stadium. The place was pretty full. Our tickets were standing but in a stand to the left. We were in. We smiled and hugged.

'I'm so excited. I can't believe that happened.'

Now, this is when the male and female species divide. By now all my internal organs had met someway in the middle of my chest and were jumping around in joyous excitement. Together they screamed, 'yeeesssss,' and were hugging each other in that male bonding way.

Jen looked at me and said, 'oh, that's a shame that those guys had split up.'

'What?' My face crumpled up in disbelief.

'The guy who sold us the tickets. His friends had split up. That's sad,' was the female reply.

I shook my head in utter disbelief. How the genders differ.

I was saved by the PA, which blasted out the first few chords of the terrific House of Pain's "Jump." The crowd, whose excitement seemed well contained, then exploded. In unison everyone was literally jumping around. Fantastic!

As the track faded, the band came on stage, followed by Bono in his black leather jacket… very cool… This lit the fuse. The roar was like at any sporting victory. Everyone screamed at once – it was deafening. For a good couple of hours we were treated to an extra-special show. The band seemed to raise the bar. Was it the last final push over the line, the thought that tonight they could sleep in their own beds or that they owed this crowd a special 'thank you'? Naomi Campbell also made an appearance. Whatever it was, this show *and* the serendipity made it very special and highly deserving of a place in my Top Gig list. I can still hear the words 'how long must I sing this song?' ringing out from the stadium.

If things had been fantastic the night before, they got even better the next day. Still buzzing with the gig highlights we decided to take a trip out to Dalkey bay to get some sea air and see the historic town. The Dart train dropped us off at small stop on top of the hill overlooking the beautiful clear sea. We walked down a few immaculate tree-lined suburban streets and admired the huge houses in the Sunday quiet. Suddenly around a corner we met a crowd of excited young folk. They were standing in front of some large black iron gates and a huge brick wall. Two very young people with a deeply serious look with walkie-talkies were watching their every move.

'Sorry, but who lives here?' I naively asked.

'Bono,' was the blunt reply.

Shocked, we stood and waited, though not really sure what we were waiting for. We weren't going to get invited in… or were we? Anything was possible following last night's lottery win. The young security folk were a bit twitchy. Suddenly down the hill came a lovely open-topped Mercedes. It was a beautiful car. The crowd weren't interested in the car. It was the single male driver wearing a bandanna that caught their eye.

It was The Edge arriving for a post-gig Sunday lunch. Here, feet away, was one of the most magnificent guitarists in the world. He smiled and waved at us. The crowd screamed.

My mouth was as wide as the Mersey Tunnel… my jaw scraping on the pavement. I was sure I was about to wake up. But no, it was really happening. The Edge gave another wave and the metal gates closed behind. That capped it. There was only one thing to do. We headed off to the pub to have a very cold Guinness. The last 24 hours had been an orgasmic musical experience. The risk and then success of getting in to see a band on top of the world playing to their home fans, and then miraculously stumbling across their home pad. Now, that was definitely a Top Gig.

As I write this I seem to be drawn to reading various recollection-themed articles. Q magazine recently carried a feature on the top six or so venues across the land. I smiled when I read the article about Brixton Academy. It mentioned the 1996 Leftfield gig I was very fortunate to attend. And it was bloody awesome.

Now, this was one hell of an event. Leftfield were a sensation when they stormed the music scene. Their first album *Leftism* was like nothing else. It was heavily bass driven, full of powerful rhythms and enriched with brilliant samples and mixes. It was capped by the star track "Open Up," featuring the one and only John Lydon. I remember hearing this track and running into Parrot Records on King Street and buying every copy in the shop… Well, it felt like that.

Unwittingly I had been searching for a new sound at this time, and Leftfield simply rode up and dropped it on the mat. I loved it. Even today I still claim it was and remains one of the best albums ever. So I had to see this band play live. During the explosion of dance came the culture of staying out late and events called all-nighters. All-nighters were gigs where venue owners somehow managed to convince their local authority to let people into their wonderful premises, drink and dance until very late – or early, depending on how you see it – into the morning. We would leave on the milk float.

Now, I wasn't so naive that I hadn't partied until the early hours but, while I loved dance music, I hadn't become a weekend clubber. It wasn't for lack of desire, it was more the pressure of having a reasonable professional job and not being a member of a heavy clubbing crowd. While we loved a good time, booze and dancing, there wasn't a strong dance culture in our crew. Leftfield, though, gave me a brilliant opportunity to try things out. With the success of *Leftism* they announced a tour that included all-nighter at Brixton. 'Brill,' I thought. 'I'm going to that.'

My ticket arrived and I went a bit crazy. By the 1990s I found myself not getting over-excited before a gig. But I was about this one. There were so many things that could make this very special. Besides hearing this legend of an album in one of the best venues in London, this was my chance to party till the sun came up.

I was well up for the gig and started to worry that I was building it up to be a Top Ten show even before the first note had been played. I always think it's better to play things down in case it fails to live up to my expectations. Once inside the Academy, though, I headed to a good central spot near the front… not too close, but central. The crowd was bustling. You could bottle the atmosphere.

This was an all-nighter, and it was already 11.00 pm. At any other event we would have been bouncing around for well over an hour, and now getting ready for the final few tracks. But tonight we'd only just come in. For three hours the crowd now 'tranced' away to a range of excellent DJs who were carefully crafting us towards the main event.

At around two in the morning, the lights finally dimmed and the last DJ moved offstage. I admit I'd yawned a few times by now, but suddenly my eyes opened fully and, with a blast of light, Leftfield appeared on stage. What happened next is now well lodged in music history. Leftfield simply reinvented the concept of bass. The first track ripped through us like a bomb. The power and sensation was like nothing I'd ever experienced. I turned around, looking for my innards at the back of the Academy along with everyone else's. I never knew sound could feel like this. It ripped our bodies open without requiring surgery. It was almost unbearable but at the same time absolutely exhilarating.

Leftfield produced an awesome gig. Track after track the crowd were lifted and gently dropped, like being on a huge trampoline or roller-coaster.

John Lydon didn't appear, but this would have put the gig into cloud cuckoo land. We left at around four in the morning. The sun was up. Very few people were around. My head was screaming, my ears ringing and my heart and lungs settling back into their rightful places in my (metaphorically) torn-apart ribcage. I had just fulfilled a dream. In a venue that deserves its own chapter I had seen the most respected new act delivering an ear-busting dance set – which turned out to be one of the most talked-about gigs in the 1990s. Brilliant! Fucking brilliant!

There are so many bands who've played excellent sets. Classy sounds, mind-blowing light shows, mesmeric journeys of sensual exploration. But only a few gigs have ever provided me with that complete package again and again and again and again. That all-inclusive package deal.

It almost feels wrong to pull out the ultra-special ones. I'm a caring person who genuinely doesn't want to cause harm. Everyone needs a chance. But in this world and culture of classifying everything, some gigs and bands deserve their own seat at the high table.

It almost goes without saying that for me the one band who consistently deliver a top show is The Cure. Their inclusion in this elite listing is based on consistency. They get a kind of Lifetime Achievement award for constant perfection. They are that one band I hate missing – which is the case when they played Bestival in the Isle of Wight in September 2011. I wasn't there. After missing them I became worryingly obsessive in wanting to get tickets to see their 2011 Royal Albert Hall show. I only found out about the event the week before. It was sold out so I had to trade hard on eBay. Luckily my enthusiasm, patience and planning paid off. I secured two quality *seats* (admittedly), but they were near the front, it was the RAH and the price was below face value. I immediately called

Richard and told him to cancel everything for next Tuesday night.

I expect that in all of us there's one band who define us. If you were ever asked to join or sign up to a life membership of this band – whether they're good, bad, sad, ugly, or even if they've 'only' played a great track – you would. Mine – after loads of heart-wrenching and heavy arguing inside my head – is probably The Cure. I've struggled for ages to understand why. I think it comes down to feeling an understanding and affinity with the band's deeper sense and direction. For what I love about The Cure is that while they put on an appearance of frivolity, of unruly madness, there's a darker side to them.

The Cure are huge, especially in France and Italy where they have a massive fan base largely on the back of their money-generating "Love Cats" single. I experienced their early work during my first gigging years – that's the music of theirs I admire most.

A band who have survived some nearly four decades have a long repertoire to draw upon. As a result there's a phase during their long sets when we head back to the mid- and early 1980s. The tone drops, the lights are virtually out and tracks such as "Primary," "M" and "At Night" ooze out of the speakers. I seem to be alone. At recent gigs I've found myself one of a handful of lost souls jumping around to these tracks. The odd teardrop forms as they hit my musical and emotional sweet spot. They remind me of a period of musical learning at an important but delicate stage of my development. I found that The Cure, while dark and slightly sinister, pulled me through.

I can genuinely say I've never seen a poor performance from Robert and his madhouse band. Even when they played the Cambridge Corn Exchange on 28 April 1992, when he announced that he had a huge self-inflicted hangover, they still managed that magic. On the basis of this, the bar is set. I dread the day The Cure disband. While over the years many bands have gone and many have re-formed, some for the better, I think that when The Cure go that will be *it*. For me this will be the ultimate challenge. If I lose my comfort blanket, what will I do? Will it be time to press Unsubscribe to all those gig-listing emails and ticket agents? I dread the day.

I feel the stress a band must experience before they come on stage. That all-important first track really can make or even destroy the evening. Now, as an impressionable youth, one band I loved but kind of feared was The Stranglers. On hearing "No More Heroes" at the age of 13 I did what most youngsters did: I put their new album on my Christmas list. I remember responding happily to my mother's enquiry as to what I'd like from Santa.

I was a bit let down when Christmas day arrived. I duly unwrapped the neatly presented gifts from Lapland only to find instead of "No More Heroes" by The Stranglers was "Heroes" by David Bowie. Maybe Santa had an age limit on explicit material for 13-year-olds. Ironically this slight misunderstanding turned out to be a good one, as "Heroes" is one of my top three tracks ever.

Anyway, back to the gigs. In 2006 The Stranglers announced a performance at the Junction in Cambridge. With no fuss, consultation or worry I got myself a ticket. By now very much less impressionable, I felt I got a reward for my years of support. With no Hugh or the rather good Paul Roberts in the line-up I was a bit nervous. I was comforted that this gig would be a bit of a homecoming. Dave Greenfield, Jet Black and Jean-Jacques Burnel all had connections to the north Cambridge area. I was sure they wouldn't let us down. The stage was suitably set with large black drapes as a backdrop. The crowd were excited. This was The Stranglers' first gig at the Junction.

The house lights went out and the crowd let out a huge roar. The band emerged through the black door to the rear and were appropriately dressed in... yep, black. In fact I don't recall any other colour in the whole venue. The line-up included Baz Warne, who had replaced the excellent John Ellis. With Jet Black (Brian Duffy) neatly ensconced behind his large black drum kit and guitars resting around the necks of Baz and the longstanding Jean-Jacques, we awaited that first note. That note from which we'd try and guess which track. That note we'd cling on to; that note which would probably set the tone for the next hour and a half.

We waited... then suddenly Jean-Jacques played that famous first note from one of most famous bass lines ever recorded.

'Din ah, din ah, din ah, din ah, din ah, din ah,' the notes cascaded out of the huge bass guitar... Within seconds the whole place was jumping around as if the floor was on fire. "No More Heroes" was blasting its way through our brains. And for full effect we were treated to a slightly extended version.

'Down the front' was a load of now mid-40s males with larger waistlines, not much hair, slightly more sober – though only just. All in our in black T-shirts too. We were in for a real pogo session. Fantastic. The evening consisted of a collection of greatest hits, all of which were belted out; we screamed them all back. 'This is what a gig is about,' I said to myself.

Now, most musos will know that Jean-Jacques is not only an extremely talented musician but also a black 6th belt in karate. A handy little sideline to have, I expect. Even though the world and virtually everyone on it has moved on since the late 1970s, some folk, while deep in reminiscence, appear to be time-warped. As gigs go this was not a violent outing. In fact it was pretty calm. I recall Hugh Cornwell stopping The Stranglers' set at Reading University in 1987 when someone spat at him. He simply told the prat that spitting had stopped years ago and he should just 'fuck off and grow up.'

Hugh was now gone. One dear muso, however, decided he was in fact back in 1978 and jumped on to the stage, somehow avoiding the security guys. For a moment this bloke thought he was in heaven. There he was on stage with The Stranglers and no one was doing anything about it. It kind of all went into slow-mo. Though the band were playing it was eerily silent for a minute. Except that Jean-Jacques had now had enough. What happened next had to be seen. Jean-Jacques took a step forward, raised his right boot and placed it under the dear muso's chin. Tap. The muso fell to the deck, completely floored. As he picked himself up and was pulled off stage the band continued to play… I can't recall which track but it didn't matter. I was slightly shocked by what I had seen. No one did a thing. 'What if JJ had connected properly?' I thought. This gig makes my Top Ten list on the basis of seeing one of my favourite punk bands nice and close-up. *And* they provided more entertainment than just classic tracks. That's rock 'n' roll. Top.

I sense there has been quite a radical change in live music over the past few years. The digital age has seen a huge growth of interest in music but the new generation have taken more to downloads and filesharing. This has meant a rapid reduction in sales of what I call hard material such as CDs. As a result we have sadly seen many bands split, many musicians gone solo or died. A few bands have kept going – good luck to them. With record sales in hard material form declining, live performance is now key to a band's success. This has been the cause of many re-emergences and apparently irrevocable re-formations.

If you had simply disappeared for the last decade and returned to Mother Earth last week you'd probably find yourself staring hard at a copy of *NME* or a billboard saying, 'what the hell? That line-up is from 1982. They can't still be around?'

Newspaper adverts, ticket agency emails and music mags are full of reunions. Pals made up. Bands back together. The unifying feature is that touring and playing live is an important way to generate music sales, particularly in new formats with additional versions, unknown B-sides and so on. I expect the target audience is their original, faithful, supporters who still yearn for those golden years but now have a bit more spare cash to re-purchase their favourite hits in some collectors' limited edition. A bit like middle-aged men buying Hornby train sets. Fair cop.

But to get to both the faithful and maybe some curious musos who missed them the first time, a band needs to tour... play live. Touring is now a lucrative business. It's great news for those of us who enjoy hearing favourite tracks in a live setting.

I make no bones about it – I've taken this opportunity to see a number of bands I missed first time around. A few are in my story. And if one of your favourite bands had re-formed, I bet *you'd* go and see them. It's a risky business, though. Can the singer still reach those high notes? Has the drummer still got the energy to keep going during a power-draining two-hour set?

If there's one band I would do a lot (i.e. probably pay a silly amount of hard cash) to see re-form, it's Cocteau Twins. There was a rumour that Liz and Robin had agreed to re-form for the Coachella Festival in the States in 2005, but this fell through. I kept alive a glimmer of hope.

Then, as if in response to my pain, I read on one of the numerous newsfeeds from one of the ticket agencies that Anthony Hegarty was organising the Meltdown Festival 2012 at the Royal Festival Hall on the South Bank, and Liz Fraser was going to play. Ok, it wasn't the full band but it was Liz and I had missed her. This was another no-brainer. I booked the tickets immediately.

It will seem quite pathetic but I was so excited about seeing Liz Fraser play again. And Liz hadn't performed live for some fourteen years. I arrived in the RFH foyer and for once visited the merchandise stall with the intention to purchase. I bought a programme, which was a very rare act.

I was early but not allowed to enter the auditorium as the support act were in mid-song. Looking about me I noticed a few other middle-aged blokes, also on their own, looking around them slightly nervously. We all seemed slightly anxious.

Just like in 1984, I was politely directed to my seat. The usherette was considerably younger this time, but the tradition hadn't changed. I valued that. I sat next to a young student who was studying singing at Edinburgh. She hadn't seen Cocteau Twins or Liz before. We chatted merrily about singing and her course. I reminded her that in her early days Liz would slap her ribs to help increase the vibrato in her voice. I was careful not to raise her expectations to the level mine were at.

I know that as I age my emotions seem more fragile. The slightest thing will put my hairs on end and make my eyes water. As Liz walked slowly across the large stage, below and in front of us, towards that one microphone in the centre at the front, I welled up. All the waiting, all the memories, all the emotions came out.

Liz started rather hesitantly. I wasn't hearing that crystal-clear vocal. I was worried. Would all the waiting and my anxieties come to a grinding halt? But on track three, her voice strengthened and was more audible. It was beautiful. It regained strength and came across balanced, ringing, clear and wonderful. For the next hour and a bit we were treated to an exemplary performance from a unique but shy artist. The classics were perfectly mixed with a number of new creations – she had obviously not been dormant over the last decade. Her backing band were magnificently supportive. Steve Hackett, ex-Genesis guitarist, also joined for a track… The gig went far too quickly. Before we knew it Liz had left the stage, only to be sucked back on by a polite adoring crowd who just wouldn't let her go. The encore and ending on its own was worth the entrance fee. We were treated to a magnificent version of Tim Buckley's "Song to the Siren," which was covered by Liz when in the musical collective called This Mortal Coil. If you haven't heard it, please go and find it and have a listen now. It might just provide a minor glimpse into the magic of Liz and why this show was worth waiting some twenty years for. For the pain of waiting and for my genuine love of this artist it has to be a Top Gig.

I just ask that I don't have to wait so long for the next one.

It isn't often that Cambridge greets a band named after a road. Orbital formed in 1989 and named themselves after the infamous M25. It represents a musical era that was literally going nowhere until they arrived. By the early 1990s the dance scene had taken off, and Orbital were at the forefront of the next music revolution.

After some fifteen years, and with many tears, Orbital declared that their 2004 gigs at the close of Glastonbury and T in the Park would be their last. The brothers Hartnoll needed some time apart. Paul went on to produce a good but not necessarily well-received album, *The Ideal Condition*.

But Orbital had unfinished business. To the delight of their many adoring fans, they re-formed in 2009 and have since produced in 2012 a new classic album titled *Wonky*. Back together, Paul and Phil Hartnoll took to the road. We were treated to a brilliant, indeed exemplary, show of dance trance on Monday night at the Corn Exchange, 9 April 2012.

Orbital are simply the masters of techno wizardry. Supported by the quality warm-up act The Japanese Pop Stars, Orbital emerged to a mammoth re-union roar. They opened with the opening track from *Wonky*, "One Big Moment," and immediately set out their stall. With a graphic artist's kaleidoscopic backdrop, the heavy but clear rhythms of their tunes soon had the Corn Exchange moving if not shaking with the bass. It was 'hands in the air and eyes closed' time – a masterclass in dance.

With each mesmerising track we were drawn closer into the Hartnolls' world of buttons, knobs and samples. While focussing on *Wonky*, we were rewarded with a remix of their classics. "Impact" was a pure delight; they took "Halcyon + On + On" to a new height, though arguably dumbed down with the sample of Belinda Carlisle's "Heaven Is A Place on Earth." Not my favourite, but certainly one the crowd liked.

The wonder of Orbital is that they do literally take you on a journey – a journey into a world of trance, solid beats and powerful driving synth. All supported by a crystal-clear backdrop light show that swirls and twirls. Corny, but it's hard not to put your hands in the air, shut your eyes and dream.

Wonky is a stonker of an album. You can feel that Phil and Paul have found their creativity again. Underlying their softer trance style are some gritty and punchy tracks such as the ear-bashing "Stringy Acid" and the roaring Prodigy-styled "Beelzedub." As the decibels exceed the pain barrier the main set closes, with the swaying crowd now 'tranced.'

The encore is a real treat, with a brilliant version of the classic "Chime," plus the final track from *Wonky*, "Where Is It Going?" – a track of pure techno genius. The perfect way to end an epic gig. This was arguably their best-ever performance. For a band already in my Top Ten, that's saying something. Genius.

Thirteen: **Rituals**

> *Zero, zero, one, one, nine*
> *'Ca Yellowman make yuh feel so fine*
> *Me chat all me lyric*
> *Me chat dem in a rhyme*
> *Me nuh eat lime it full of a rhyme*
> *'Ca Yellowman him a commit nuh crime,*
>   *'ca*
>
> **"Zungguzungguguzungguzeng" by Yellowman**

I'M NOT VERY SUPERSTITIOUS but I seem to have adopted a set of rituals when going to a gig.

This is not like going to a football game, which has become weirdly obsessive. Sporting rituals are different and very complex. At football I won't risk anything. The pattern is set. Get train, meet my mates, go to pub, have a pint or maybe two, walk to ground, enter ground through Gate 2, buy programme, watch game, leave ground and (having lost) think, 'what on earth did I do to break the ritual?'

The crucial difference with gigs is that the impact of not following a set ritual is not going to affect the end result. The worst case is that the gig will have been cancelled and you weren't told. That did happen to me in the 1990s when Tricky had a car accident and the Massive Attack gig at the Corn Exchange was cancelled. And Tim Booth from James was ill and called off his UEA gig in October 1991. But 9.9 times out of 10 the band will turn up and play their planned set.

Not like football. Break even the simplest element of an

established routine and you will make the team lose, casting you down into a day of torture and torment. 'Oh my God. It was all my fault. I bought sweets from that stall outside the ground. I knew I shouldn't have. They tasted rubbish and we lost 1–0.' Utter rubbish, of course, but I bet you're thinking, 'er, yes… When I think about it I do seem to have a set routine when I go to a sporting event.'

My current routine for local gigs is quite simple. It follows a pattern: Put kids to bed, jump in car, park near the Backs, walk across Garrett Hostel Lane Bridge, admire the beautiful Trinity Hall Library next to bridge, cross Market Square, pick up tickets, get hand stamped, smile at the security guy collecting tickets (we're on smiling and greeting terms now), enter foyer, buy a drink and head into the stalls section. All very straightforward.

The thing is, many of my friends don't follow this routine. For a number of them, going to a gig is a serious night out. They leave home at six and pop into to the pub for a few beers before going into the venue. Interestingly, not many go for food… gigs aren't theatre shows. You don't see the kebab van or chip shop offering pre-gig dinner sittings.

Food, I find, is often neglected, or is certainly not a priority. Food is the post-gig activity. In my typical routine I get home and raid the bread bin and snack cupboard. Paul and the Cambridge crew have an unmoveable ritual of always seeking out some dodgy takeaway after a gig. Over recent years – since Paul (now my ex-neighbour) and I discovered we had a joint fascination for music, especially bands from the 1980s – Paul and I have been going to gigs as kind of unit. Paul, Ralph, Rich and Stan are long-term schoolmates who, like me, have signed up to years of listening to indie bands across the land.

Our common bond has to be one of the strangest – we all have a fascination for Killing Joke. Now, Killing Joke are not your average band by any stretch, as you will have heard earlier. In fact they're probably one of those bands you've either never heard of, hate or adore. Many huge bands in their own right, such as Nine Inch Nails, Gary Numan and Andy Cairn's Therapy?, refer to them as an influence. We fall into the adoration group. We've probably seen them on every tour since their reunion in 1988. Killing Joke are fronted by Jaz Coleman, who is a musical genius but frighteningly on the edge of being sectioned. Infamously in 1982, before playing an eagerly awaited small tour in those dodgy venues across the country, he went AWOL and was found somewhere in Iceland.

I'll tell you later how I found out about Paul's and my shared musical tastes, but for now I'll just say that Paul invited me to join him and his friends at a Killing Joke reunion gig at London's (now demolished) Astoria venue.

The Astoria gig was a brilliant performance of power and pure aggression. The five of us arrived in good time, which is part of Paul's ritual. He likes to arrive early. It was important to follow this rule at the Astoria as after a gig it would become a nightclub, so we were all pushed out well before 10:30 to get the club up and running. Bands could often appear on stage before the traditional nine o'clock start. We entered the tiny theatre-like venue. Having bought the customary beer we positioned ourselves in a row a few feet from the back. We all agreed the support band were awful and that this seems to be a theme with Killing Joke gigs. The support band seem to be selected on the basis that they are appalling. If they upstage or threaten KJ's status they risk being locked in the dressing room and all the occupants sent to the very bowels of hell and/or the flames of Armageddon, both of which feature in most KJ tracks.

I hadn't been to a Killing Joke gig for a few years, although about twelve of us had seen them at the V Festival – rather a surprise package there – in Chelmsford in 2003. Tonight, Jaz, Geordie and Paul were on fine form. Heavy and angry, they started with a few classics. I was immediately drawn in. On the Third Track I made my move – within a few seconds I was down the front surrounded by some very large, very bald and very menacing faces. I could touch Jaz's black boots and green jump suit. We all screamed "Wardance" back to the boiler-suited and black-eyelined Jaz as he glared at us. Tonight was almost a greatest hits event, if Killing Joke could ever claim to have a set of greatest hits. As long-term followers we were certainly treated to plenty of firm favourites.

At the end of this crazy show, having probably bashed and jumped for over an hour, I walked back to find Paul and the crew. This was my first trip to a gig with Paul and his pals. Most of my gig-going mates are members of the 'down the front' posse. The venue was by now quite empty. There, near the back, Paul, Ralph, Rich and Stan were stood in a line. Exactly the same line as when we had arrived. They looked at me up and down. I was now drenched in sweat.

We left the venue and headed off at Paul's behest to find a decent (if possible) takeaway. Just around the corner we descended upon some small fast-food joint and ordered a variety of things described as 'food.' I was still dripping in sweat and decided to take off my black T-shirt. I handed it to Paul while I put on the other top I had sensibly brought with me. Paul looked at me in disgust and held the sodden fabric at arm's length, threatening to leave it in the takeaway.

This was our cross-over of rituals. I love going down the front and jumping around for an hour; Paul wants his takeaway.

I've never been a major merchandise collector. It kind of goes with my lack of fashion consciousness. I always felt most of the official gear is too expensive. By the time the gig has ended I'm usually out of cash. In plenty of cases I'm thinking the gig was fine but I don't need some Motorhead-emblazoned pants. While getting my hands on a set list is a real bonus, I do my collecting by buying music. As a vinyl record collector the thing I do look out for is limited edition albums, coloured vinyl, gatefold sleeves, different sleeve colours – *Do It Yourself* by Ian Dury came out in no less than 12 different covers. CDs with additional tracks are quite tempting. At some gigs you can pick up some great gems. I find local and new bands score well in this regard. I've often picked up debut albums from new bands for less than shop prices – and there's sometimes the chance of the band signing it. Real groupie stuff, I admit. This is when you can get to meet the artists – while human and often shy, I notice they're regularly quite small in stature. Cara Dillon, Lucy Rose and Thea Gilmore are examples.

There have been a couple of times when I've succumbed to the additional commercial pressures at gigs. In fact Jez very kindly bought me a Cocteau Twins T-shirt following their stonking show at the Cambridge Corn Exchange in February 1994. I still have the T-shirt but for some reason it has shrunk, so it doesn't come out of the loft very often.

It's also part of the ritual to look at the counterfeit T-shirts you usually find being sold by blokes dressed in black outside venues across the land. These shirts are significantly cheaper but obviously poorer quality than the band's own merchandise. These fakes (which in some cases are hoodies, as they have become trendier over recent years) usually consist of some iconic band or album logo and a list of tour dates on the back. They're nothing special in my eyes, though I did buy two James T-shirts following a brilliant gig at the UEA in Norwich. A blue one for me and a pink one for my Australian niece Lucy. (It was her first gig, having stepped in for Jen, who was not feeling well.) Following their Birmingham gig I recently succumbed to buying a bright red James T-shirt complete with flower logo. Lots of my friends buy merchandise this way, though I never see them wearing it afterwards. Funny that.

Some bands take this illicit trading very seriously – it's theft. I realise why the sellers are always dressed in black, wearing trainers and always on edge. They remind me of those bootleg traders you get in most international cities selling fake handbags and sunglasses. With the dream of the reward, there's the risk of being caught by the band's own security. I've heard it rumoured they don't handle these things in a very libertarian way. Post-gig bashings have been heard of.

I recall going in to a Depeche Mode gig in Birmingham and hearing a few loud shouts outside. Suddenly I saw a young lad with a bag of merchandise being bundled to the ground by a few very large, determined and burly bouncers. The young lad, fearing for his life, dropped the bag and pegged it into the crowd. The loss of his stock seemed preferable to the retribution the bouncers clearly had in mind.

I digress, but having not seen Depeche Mode for some years I wasn't too sure what to expect. Often the best way to be, because this was a really brilliant show. Yes a show but unbelievably brilliant. Capped off by them playing "Never Let me Down" as an encore with the whole crowd vigorously swaying our arms side to side, instructed by Dave Gahan, like being in some Jane Fonda workout. Bloody brilliant. Anyway…..

At the large events with those bands that have, as it were, 'made it,' you can even give up another twenty odd quid on a tour programme. I often look at these programmes before an event, simply to see what on earth is being offered. Too often they're just a collection of in-focus live photographs with a couple of pages of commentary. But in truth that's about it. Twenty quid?

Festival programmes are much more interesting, primarily as they tell you who's playing and when. Very helpful, I find. They always have positive write-ups of the bands. Interestingly, over the years the content and quality of programmes has increased. With the old ones it's a bit like comparing a Blue Square League programme with that of a Premier League club. While I'm not keen on bands' programmes, unless they're at special events, I notice many are now trading at good prices as collectors' items. I need to check this out in more detail. Maybe this part of the ritual needs a review.

What I want at a gig is some collectable, cheap, signed album. Some bands now use the captive audience opportunity to sell CDs, and a few bands *do* offer limited editions. My local favourites Ezio always have a good stock their albums. The beauty is that immediately after their performance Ezio and Booga will appear and happily sign any merchandise or body part offered to them… as long as you have a good marker pen. A tip to remember.

A few bands have also taken up the idea of offering post-event live recordings, which is rather smart I feel. However, while I often want a souvenir of a memorable event, I'm always let down by live recordings. There are plenty of exceptions. The first is Roxy Music's *Viva* album. It was recorded in a buoyant Newcastle City Hall and brilliantly captures what must have been an amazing gig.

James produced a live CD set of 2008 shows, to which I decided I would treat myself as a memento. I was shocked recently to find out these are now trading at some three-figure sum.

In the early days we didn't have iPhones and the surprisingly sophisticated DIY equipment capable of producing near-studio-quality recordings. All we had were bootleg tapes, most of which were of appalling quality. I vividly remember standing (of course) next to some bloke at a gig who spent the whole show holding his small Dictaphone at head height, taping. Can you imagine how awful that will have sounded? But back then, musos would trade hard-earned cash for these poor, hardly recognisable recordings. Yes, I have a few.

I've always admired the arty-farty side of the 4AD label and its bands. Everything about 4AD is class. The album artwork is carefully designed and worthy of any gallery. This was the home both of the fabulous Cocteau Twins and one of the most amazing bands I've ever heard: Dead Can Dance. Now, Dead Can Dance are unique. They have created some truly brilliant songs, built around ancient medieval folk songs. They manage to combine these with the wonderful vocals of Lisa Gerrard and Brendan Perry. While I was at Oxford Poly I was given a copy of their *Serpent's Egg* album by Alex in the Ents team. It wasn't his thing, and Dead Can Dance sadly wouldn't be appearing on the term roster. But I revelled in their inspiring recordings.

Dead Can Dance weren't prolific tourers. I never saw them live until 2005 when they, partly re-formed, played at the Town and Country Club. While most gigs I go to are raucous, this show was noticeable for its attention to detail. Every note was perfectly performed. Even the silence was beautifully respected. While I tried hard to store away my images and memories of this wonderful set, the great news was that the band decided to record every gig – and issued a series of CDs with a set of limited edition live recordings. These recordings used sophisticated technology to give studio-quality sound while keeping the live ambiance. Now collectable, these are some of the best live recordings I own.

But there's one ritual I uphold to quite embarrassing extremes. Gig tickets are off the scale. They're the cause of many arguments at home. I've managed to keep very nearly a complete set of gig tickets. I have the ticket from virtually every single gig, event or festival I've been to – except for about a half a dozen. One I haven't got is the Random Hold gig at the old Marquee Club. That was because the ticket was more appropriate for a cinema. Also the meathead bouncer gave me that 'fuck off you geek, what do you want that piece of crap for?' look… I was a bit too innocent and young to argue. Also I didn't want to miss the gig so I didn't push it. Bastard!

But how tickets have changed! You can occasionally get a well-decorated and well-designed ticket, but so many now are depressingly boring. Many are simply computer printouts that look more like supermarket receipts than anything relating to a gig. Right from the start I decided I would keep all my tickets, and I'm pleased to report this remains a now-obsessional imperative. I'll go to bizarre lengths to get tickets. On the odd occasion I haven't been able to keep to my plan, but this has been rare.

I thought I was alone with this weird hoarding fixation. But I've found out that many musos do the same. Right from the start of my 'down the front' journey I've carefully put the gig ticket away in a safe place. After a few years I had established such a good collection of quality tickets that I decided to frame them. Over the years I've become a shareholder in those cheap clip frames you get from Habitat and so on. Well, I managed to fill about four large frames by the mid-1980s.

My school pal and early gig-going pal Tim also built up a good collection and framed his too. They became good talking points over the years.

I mentioned earlier that a previous neighbour of mine, Paul, is also a muso. I found this out one sunny day while gardening when I heard Paul playing Cocteau Twins. He hadn't long moved in. I nearly stabbed my foot with the spade in surprise. Now, no disrespect to my other neighbours but I've never ever had one who was a muso, and certainly never one who had heard and played the beautiful Cocteau Twins. It isn't often you hear the luxurious harmonies of my favourite band drifting over the cheap fence panels separating our abodes. A few days later we did that new neighbour thing. While standing in our respective front doorways we started to chat over the small wooden fence at the front.

'Sorry to ask, but I heard you playing Cocteau Twins the other day,' I said precisely. I wanted to make the point early of knowing the proper name of the band.

'Oh yeah, great band. Do you like them?' Paul asked.

'Like them? I almost went on tour with them, I loved them so much,' I replied.

'Do you go to many gigs?' he enquired.

'Probably too many. I always have. What about you?'

'Yeah, me and lots of schoolmates go. In fact we're planning to see Killing Joke next year.'

I nearly fell over said fence.

'What? You like Killing Joke?' I nearly choked.

'Always have done,' he said.

'Bloody hell. I'm a huge fan. Saw them in the early 1980s in

Reading. The Top Rank Club. I've still got the ticket,' was my still-shocked reply.

'You know, I collect mine as well. I keep them in a frame.'

With that Paul invited me in and proceeded to show me his ticket collection. I studied it closely.

'I was at that one, and that one, and that one. That gig was awesome,' I recalled. So here we were, two reasonably sensible middle-aged men with very little hair between us, sharing gig memories over ticket stubs.

I was kind of relieved by this bizarre meeting of neighbours. Here, next door, was someone on his own musical journey, virtually on the same lines as mine. I suddenly felt a bit less of a freak. This music thing had at least one more nutter. Another nutter who also had his rituals.

But I have one ritual that, I believe, is pretty unique. It started way back in the mid-1980s. We had had a brilliant day at Milton Keynes Bowl listening to the amazing David Bowie at his best.

This was the 'Serious Moonlight' tour. It seems that everyone I knew was there. I digress a bit but ironically I later found out that I knew even more people here than I had thought. Within hours of arriving at Oxford Poly I met Nic and Stu. We soon found ourselves recalling all the gigs we had seen and finding out we had been to many of the same ones. I showed them a picture taken at the Bowie gig at Milton Keynes Bowl. Stu stared at the photo and suddenly screamed, 'fuck. Look. That's me.' And he was right, in the near background you could see Stu and some young girl sitting on the bank, like us, waiting for Bowie to make our day.

Anyway Bowie had attracted a great crowd, and we spent the afternoon lying on the bank soaking up the sun, drinking, eating, laughing and enjoying life. The support acts, The Beat and Icehouse, did their job wonderfully. The crowd was buzzing, really chatty, many singing throughout.

Bowie was incredible. We poured out of the Bowl with "Modern Love" tingling our ears. We returned to the car and then got stuck in one of those painful traffic queues you get at end of a large show. All you want to do is get home. After a gig my mind wafts away. I keep trying to play it all back. I'm trying to push the best bits deep into the vast memory bank somewhere in my music-filled head.

Our crowd were laughing and full of themselves. Suddenly I hear Bowie's voice radiate out from a car stereo nearby. It distracts me. I start to lose the memory and the sound from the show. Like a disappearing ghost or the rising of a deep mist. My brain is ruffled. It's confused. It doesn't know what to record and preserve. It closes down.

'No way,' I call out. 'I don't want to hear Bowie now,' I tell my crowd. They give each other slight questioning glances. I don't think they get it. 'Turn it off!' I yell. 'I want to be able to remember the concert. I don't want to hear anything by the artist I've just seen. It takes everything away. If you want to hear the album stay at home. Don't lose the moment,' I ranted. Speech over, our crowd went quiet. We wound up the windows in an attempt to block out the sound. We put one of my compilation tapes on ERD's stereo and turned it up. It helped. A bit.

From that day I decided that seeing a gig is so important that I must, no matter what, preserve the memory of it. I made a deal with myself that evening. My dual personality organised a meeting. We came, we met and we shook hands. We agreed from then on I would hold a polite truce for three days. For the next 72 hours I would deliberately not play anything by the band I had just seen. Mad, yes. But for me it's a ritual I stand by. For me it works. The excitement I get three days later when the curfew is lifted is immense. I swear I'm able to go directly back to the gig in fully live Technicolor and hear it just how it was performed. For this reason alone it's worth it. It's my ritual and it works.

Fourteen: **The Final One**

> *'Cause holy cow / I love your eyes*
> *And only now I see you like / Yeah,*
> *lying with me half awake,*
> *Stumbling over what to say / Well,*
> *anyway,*
> *It's looking like a beautiful day*
>
> **"One Day Like This" by Elbow**

THEY ALWAYS COME IN THREES, GIGS. Like waiting for the proverbial bus, you can go weeks and even months without seeing a live band, then suddenly three come along. In the spring of 2012 I had a classic example of a muso's week in live music. It started with having to duck out of the Monday night footy in favour of seeing the up-and-coming Lucy Rose play at the Portland Arms... before it was refurbished.

I had briefly seen Lucy when she played supporting vocals and the odd violin bit for Bombay Bicycle Club on their recent visit to Cambridge. Lucy follows that wonderful trend of petite, attractive young females who speak with northern accents but sing like angels. Her gig in the back room of the Portland Arms was sold out. On a rare warm early summer evening we crammed into the tiny room with its peeling black paint and the odd poster on the still smoke-tarred walls.

A few static stage lights hung from the ceiling. The glitter ball swung with the movement of warm sweaty air. The crowd was a mixed bag. Young trendy students mixed with us oldies. Together we were quietly reserved and had to be asked, if not ordered, by the sound engineer to move closer to the stage to ensure that everyone could get in. Rob was with me but Jez was ill. He'd miss out.

Lucy has the looks of the early Toyah. She is quietly confident and delivers a series of lovely ballads supported by a great band of musicians. While mainly folky, what I admire most is how Lucy manages to drop into a range of styles and themes. One track was constructed around three different rhythms before it settled into another swaying melody. I felt like that glitter ball, gently wafting in the caring breeze.

I didn't know any of her material and had simply attended on a subliminal instinct that this would be a great evening. And I was right. It was perfect.

Wednesday saw me go back to the Junction to see the one band whose second album, for nearly twelve months – well, certainly a whole summer – I played so much I wore it out. He was never everyone's cup of char, but I found his sound unique and powerful, while dark and a bit weird. In his early days he was a peroxide blond who only wore customary indie black clobber. Now the peroxide is black – some musos claim it is in fact a wig.

Gary Numan has been one of those distinctive artists who, against his critics, has stayed loyal to his game. In my first year in Oxford I went to see Tubeway Army play at the Apollo. I couldn't find anyone at all to join me. But I wasn't put off. I had half expected to arrive and be given the choice of every seat in the house. Luckily for Gary a fair-sized crowd had gathered. We witnessed a classic set of electronic futuristic indulgences supported by loads of dazzling light effects.

In 2009 Gary returned to playing a few smaller venues, which had included our Junction. He played a storming gig. His music had got heavier over the years, having added a set of guitar sounds to those well-crafted electro chords. I remember coming out of the gig thinking, 'fucking hell, that was great. The sound just went into another dimension.' The final track was "Prayer for the Unborn," which was simply on another plane. Bloody brilliant… and check out the lyrics.

I was intrigued to see if he could pull it off again. I must have banged on about the previous gig a lot because even football pal Paul decided to come along. The Junction was rammed. Even the sneaky move from the main bar to the other side of the auditorium was hard. The crowd were mainly middle-aged musos with fewer follicles between all of us than under Gary's (alleged) wig. Black was the colour, although I rebelled and resorted to a Glasto-styled T-shirt. I was sure Gary wouldn't mind. We stood near the back, far to the side. This was the first night I decided to wear my new ear protectors.

Over the last few years I've started to suffer from a slight tinnitus in my left ear. I've tried to manage it at gigs by standing more on the right side or using mushed up paper as a block; sometimes I've tried, in vain, to clear the inevitable feeling of blockage by regularly yawning or clearing my throat. All of which has been like saying, 'I'll learn to play the piano without having a piano.' Bloody useless.

So one day I decided I'm not giving up this gig lark. I still want that feeling of freedom. I still want to see bands and come home saying 'I was there.' I went to Millers music shop and bought some acoustic ear plugs. I chose the medium-priced ones that look like a miniature set of those electric connectors you see on pylons or in the futuristic art park in the Shangri-La at Glastonbury.

I nervously took them out of their neat little carry case and pushed them delicately into my damaged ears. I was expecting a rush of sarcasm from my mates and those around me, or – to my horror – being pulled out from the crowd, spotlighted, stoned and banned from every venue in the land. But nothing. Not a word.

Numan took to the stage with his fellow band members, all of whom had that real band member look. Have you ever noticed that? There are some musicians that look… well, just like… very real and well-travelled band members rather than nervous fresher students. Numan's band are the former. They were dressed in the customary black jeans, with manicured spikey hair and dark T-shirts with some obscure but compelling logo. They looked the real deal.

The gig itself was fine but didn't have the same impact as in 2009. Numan's live shows are supported by a range of artistic video footage played on huge screen behind the band. There was a different video for each song, ranging from a close-up of a woman's mouth with bright red lips to a collage of snippets of wars and the terrorist attack on the Twin Towers. The set list was a collection of greatest chart hits, but it was the classics "Down in the Park" and "Are Friends Electric?" that stood out. There's a heavier edge to Numan's music these days, with a greater use of guitars, which I like, in support of the traditional electronic keyboard. The new sound is epitomised by the excellent and standout track "A Prayer for the Unborn" which was played more mid-set this time. Check it out.

It also sounded fine through my ear protection. Still heavy, still provocative. Paul, though, wasn't impressed. 'I could have just come for the last two songs,' he said dismissively.

Friday was another jump in scale. This time it was down to London to see Coldplay at the self-styled 'Home of Football': Emirates Stadium. Now, there are certain bands who can perform on large stages and those who can't. I've always thought that Coldplay are a band of scale and maturity who can play large – just.

I first saw Coldplay perform at the V Festival in Chelmsford. It was 2000, and "Yellow" was gaining a lot interest. Even back then, Chris Martin and pals created a new and interesting sound; they had something about them. They could draw the crowd in. As predicted by the various media pundits, Coldplay have gone global, producing a series of brilliant, popular songs. I've seen them play a number of times – much to the dismay of Stu, who absolutely hates them. He hates them so much I've been threatened with a physical beating on plenty of occasions. The only thing that saves me is my threat to expose his membership of the merry band of Morris dancers. *Touché*.

Jenny decided to take up the offer to see Coldplay, which was a surprise – maybe it was because her local choir had been learning "Viva La Vida." It presented us with one of those rare chances in our Outnumbered Family to catch up with each other. While I eagerly awaited an inspirational chat about new work opportunities and how well the children are getting on, the whole journey seemed to be taken up phone calls and or sending tweets. God! I know why I go to gigs alone.

I was also intrigued to see if the so-called 'Home of Football' could, in fact, become a music venue as well as a mecca to quality attacking football not usually seen outside Barcelona. Ok, I'll rephrase that last bit... a music venue as well as a mecca to a stubborn Frenchman's desire to play quality football with insufficient resources and a group of players whose egos are larger than Chris Martin's. That's more like it.

After a lovely dinner of Turkish/Kurdish origin we headed to the ground. I recalled my early footballing journeys and recounted memories of a young boy entering the man's world of football culture, seeing pitched gang fights, watching the ticket touts, hearing the chants, feeling the excitement. Our journey to Emirates Stadium followed parts of a previously well-trodden route of years ago. While much of the area has been redeveloped, the roads are the same and they hold ancient and precious memories.

We entered the ground through my usual turnstile. The same stewards stood in their familiar places as on match days. For a second I thought I was going to see a match. The fabulous green pitch was covered in a hard white plastic mat, and Marina and the Diamonds were pulling every sinew to entertain the growing crowd. Marina did well. She marched across the stage in her ballroom dress while singing her heart out. Her journey symbolically followed my week. A month ago Marina and the Diamonds graced our Junction; now she was here at the Emirates, just a white dot on the enormous stage.

Sadly, the Kurdish dinner meant we'd missed Ash – the stage show times said they would be on second. 'Damn. I wanted to see them,' I cried out.

Later than timetabled, in a dimming daylight, the whole place suddenly went dark. The typical scream from the crowd resonated round the vast stadium. A series of large circular screens lit up, and the four dots became recognisable. Although we were standing, we could take cover from the rain near the back. We had a great view of the stage set but it made the band virtually invisible life-size. Sadly the event was devoid of atmosphere.

Coldplay have an extraordinarily large following, and it was great to sit back and people-watch. Besides the typical young couples who, I'd suggest, only went to see a couple of gigs per year, there were young professionals from a range of backgrounds, the odd family, a few oldies and some same-sex couples. There seemed to be lots of hugging going on. A lot of the crowd were in largish groups who would suddenly link arms and dance around like at a wedding. Blokes would be walking down the aisles and suddenly throw both arms in the air as if someone had scored.

Coldplay appeared to be on form and treated us to a journey through their classics. Chris Martin engaged us while Jonny Buckland performed plenty of wizardry with his guitar. The crowd lapped it up. A key part of a Coldplay show is the stage techniques. Besides the gold ticker tape, the huge heart-shaped balloons and the large bouncy ball that gets passed, beach-style, around the sides, tonight we were in for a real first.

On entry to the stadium we were handed a coloured wristband. Midway into the show, once night had snuffed out the day, we were instructed by Chris to put our hands in the air. All the wristbands started flashing at the same time. The whole stadium was lit up with thousands of small waving Christmas lights. It was an amazing sight. I was impressed.

The other trick they pull off is usually before the final track. The band leave the safety of the main stage and head down to the back, reappearing amongst the crowd on a small intimate stage to play a couple of acoustic tracks. Again I'm impressed, as they seem to recognise that, while wanting to fill a vast stadium, there has to be an intimacy with their fans.

We charged forward to this mini stage to take in this rather private gig. The acoustic set demonstrates the strength of their songs. Chris and the band say farewell and head back to the main stage. Meanwhile I notice a guy in a white suit and a green trilby playing a blow-up guitar in full high-pitched solo mode. I smile. The guy gets loads of attention and looked happy as Larry (whoever *he* was). With encore complete we leave and speed out of the ground over the Ken Friar Bridge, surrounded by an impromptu crowd sing-along.

On the way home I play back the week. Three very different gigs, bands, venues and emotions. To be fair, each one had its highlights. Each one had its downsides, and none troubled my Top Ten. But this is what it's all about. As a gig-going muso I felt invigorated by a week of live music. I felt re-energised. I wanted to push on with my life. I started dreaming up new ideas, new businesses, and new projects. The music had re-entered my veins and I was flush with excitement. This was why I love music. It's more than a part of me, it's my life.

Well, that's it. Over the years I've been very privileged to have seen and been able to afford to see some fantastic gigs. I've been to a variety of venues, seen a million flashing light effects, listened to plenty of support acts, drunk gallons of crap beer and had my ears blasted out on hundreds of occasions. It's now time to take a break.

Or is it?

Fifteen: **Encore**

> *I could be the catalyst that sparks the revolution*
> *I could be an inmate in a long-term institution*
>
> **"What a Waste" by Ian Dury and the Blockheads**

'I can't leave now,' I call out to my new-found friends.

'They're bound to come back.'

There's always the tradition of an encore. Well, in most cases. Wikipedia suggests that an encore originates from the bleeding obvious word *encore*, meaning 'again.' It signifies the spontaneity of the audience applauding while demanding more.

In the golden early days, gigs weren't as militarily planned as they are today. Everything, now, is under contract, times are set, and the curfew means that even heavyweights such as Springsteen and McCartney get the plug pulled on them. But before this strategic planning came into force, bands would no doubt have a set list and some sense of order. In many ways you had to, otherwise you'd start playing a different song at the wrong time, which in some cases might sound better than Lou Reed's noise thing I mentioned in chapter 7.

Gigs were shorter in my early days. They had to be. New bands had limited repertoires. This was also the period of the three-minute pop song. In the early 1980s you could cram plenty of them into a gig of no more than an hour.

The encore was often a genuinely earned treat. For both parties. We used to play a guessing game of which track they would play. I can recall a few bands replaying a hit they had performed expertly in the main set. But now everything is much more planned and, as a result, diminishes the excitement of the encore. Or does it?

There's a routine to this encore thing. In most cases the lead singer ends the main set, tired but still buzzing on the adrenaline, waving and reaching one more time for the microphone. 'Thank you and good night,' he or she calls. Or, as Robert Smith regularly says, something sounding more like '*Queue.*'

At this point the crowd gather a deep breath and scream out, 'more! We want more.' A few might be cruder. 'Come back you fat twat,' I've heard a few folk shout out.

For others you get the repeat name chant. Like 'Elvis, Elvis, Elvis.' Then there are the direct request ones such as, 'we want more, we want more.' Rather boring, I'd suggest. There are also the football chant ones like 'Olé, olé, olé, olé, olé.'

But the classic and probably the most alluring is the patient slow handclap, which starts off quietly and, like some classical opera, builds to a rapid crescendo. These don't happen now as often as they did in the 1980s. The crowds are different now, and so (with respect) are many of the bands. I used to love starting off the slow handclap. I would only do this if I had enjoyed the show. I didn't do this for any of the bands in chapter 7, I can assure you.

Bands approach the encore in a variety of ways. For some it's simply part of the gig. They walk off, we clap, and they come back. What, almost, is the point?

Some bands are more direct, and do the 'now, look, we haven't got long. We're going to go off, have a fag and then we'll be back' thing. Or there are those that signal 'it's that encore time. Look, make out we're leaving, we'll just pop off backstage for a second, you clap and we'll come back on. Is that alright?'

I've witnessed Tim Booth end James' main set with "Sometimes," with the crowd screaming the lyrics back at volume ten. He waved and applauded as he and his brilliant band headed off. The Birmingham crowd had been immense. We hadn't stopped singing all night. And even though the stage was empty, we weren't giving up. Still in full song, we screamed back, '*sometimes, when I look into your eyes I can see your soul.*' As we got louder and the clapping became explosive, Tim and crew reappeared. They paused for a few seconds, looked at Tim, simply picked up their instruments and simply continued where they had left off. Fantastic. What an encore!

Full credit to those bands who don't come back, such as the brilliant Manic Street Preachers. All the times I've seen them they've played a well-focussed guitar-driven set, with James Dean Bradfield singing his guts out. I never understand or hear a clear word all night but that doesn't matter. They end the main set with some classic like "Design for Life," slam down the guitars, wave and walk off. Never to return, until the next gig. Top marks, chaps.

Other bands are more traditional and focus on playing their greatest or most popular for an encore. That's fair enough. We punters and musos pay a lot to see bands and we do expect to hear that number one hit, or one of our more obscure favourites. If played well enough it becomes that abiding memory… until the next time. It's that unissued ticket to the next show.

Some bands are brave and go for obscurity. U2, with Bono recovered from his back injury, ended their highly anticipated headliner set at Glastonbury with "Out of Control." For those of us who had kind of grown up with the band that took over the world, we recognised and welcomed this dip into their origins. While jumping for joy, I noticed that many around me were silent and static. I expect this track wasn't to be found in their record collection. Nor on the shuffle of their iPhone.

Importantly, the encore is that time to say 'thank you,' 'farewell' and 'good night.' Bands are experienced enough to know these few tracks can make or break the gig. Some reserve their best to last.

Elbow, now famous and probably quite rich, find themselves imprisoned in the expectation trap of having one of the best anthem songs. Theirs is the passionate "One Day Like This." It's one of those brilliant songs that gives you hope, life, a reason. It simply lifts the heart and soul. I've seen Guy and crew deliver this track plenty of times now, and every time I see men singing it louder than any footy song or the national anthem. Billy Connolly once suggested we should replace our turgid national anthem with the theme from *The Archers*; I say why not replace it with "One Day Like This"? That would bring us together and we'd defeat anyone in the world. We might even win a penalty shoot-out.

I have a lot of respect for Elbow. In fact I owe them big time.

I know it'll seem like I'm trying to ride the popular bet, the odds-on favourite with only one runner. That isn't the case. I knew a bit about the band before they performed their triumph at the Brit Awards back in 2008. I remember watching the show live, which is rare for me, as I don't get off on big TV award shows.

Anyway, before the awards were held, Elbow had already announced a short UK tour, and it included the Corn Exchange.

The gig was in the early autumn. By the time I decided to go it was sold out. It also came at an emotionally difficult time for me. I expect we all go through periods when we're feeling lost, confused, and needing to regain control. I was lost.

My wobble ended up with me seeking some support and advice, but I found that hard. I wasn't used to opening up to anyone, especially another human being – it was irrelevant that I never knew them. As I got deeper into the support thing I started to reject it even more, even though I knew I had to get my act together.

The Elbow gig was on a Monday, my normal footy night with the veterans. I decided not to go to that, and I'd try my luck to get in on the night. My therapy session had been painful. Maybe it was working but it wasn't producing any answers. I ambled across town that cold evening. Cambridge was quiet. The students weren't yet back. A few voices echoed around Trinity Street. My head was spinning but I kept a low profile. I wasn't ready to meet anyone and engage in polite chitty-chat.

In one instant my luck changed. I managed to get a returned ticket, and it was standing. I followed the routine: hand stamped, nice smile, bought a pint (with added shot), showed my palm to the ultraviolet scanner and entered the downstairs arena. I felt calmer. I was in familiar surrounds and looking forward to hearing Elbow.

Guy Garvey has got such a warm persona. He comes on stage in his big-hearted way, stretches out his long arms and gives us all a huge northern hug. Tonight I felt it was personal. Here, in my venue, I felt he perceptively knew his show would do more than get a few of us singing his everyday life stories. Tonight I needed him to stretch out and let his songs grab me by the balls and throw me from wall to wall.

'Is everyone alright?' Guy asked.

My eyes welled. I choked.

I listened intently to "Tower Crane Driver," laughed at "The Fix" and cried during "One Day Like This." It was the best tonic I could ever have asked for. It felt like a show just for me.

I felt fitter and stronger as I meandered my way out, picking up a few spare tickets. Maybe it sounds pathetic, perhaps crass, but this gig had given me an injection. The one that's labelled, 'Pull yourself together. Get back to the real you.'

In just over 130 minutes of live music, wonderfully performed, nicely engineered, and graciously delivered, I began to wake up. This is what I needed. I couldn't engage with the self-analysis, being lectured, and counselled. What I need was a gig that would let me dissolve and then re-form. Live music was my saviour, my spliff, my valium.

While Guy sings about striking off the PM for not replying to his invitation, I'm writing to Guy to thank him. He unwittingly brought me home. Thank you.

Sixteen: **The Bonus Track**

And I would search everywhere just to hear your call
And walk upon stranger roads than this one
I give to you my soul
I miss you more

"Afterglow" by Genesis

I LOOKED AT MY PHONE. It was saying a couple of minutes to eleven. Curfew time. This would be their last song. Another gig over. Another experience to log. Another notch on the musical bedhead. Plenty of things to remember and record for the musical reference library in my brain.

But what would the last track be? If you were in a band, what would you end with?

I'd argue that the last track, like the last page of a book is, if anything, more important than the first. Those last few chords, that final wave goodbye, the final chorus – they're what everyone will carry in their heads as they leave the warm venue and re-enter the cold real world outside. If the band get this one track wrong it could ruin the show and their reputation. You might never buy anything by them again. If they get it right you'll lead the singing into the market square and someone will hear *your* echo as they order chips from the kebab van.

When I started this book I had a weekend seeing a couple of gigs. This was in December 2011. It kind of epitomises why I love gigs. To many people, seeing two gigs in a weekend is outrageous. But life for a muso isn't straightforward. Along my journey I've often found that gigs often come together in twos or threes. My record is three gigs in three nights. Not a world record, I know – Hugo did a 365 - beat that – but it's probably enough. It's enough to soak up, enough to remember and enough to afford.

This gig weekend involved seeing two very different gigs, both at the Cambridge Corn Exchange.

The Saturday night gig was the turn of the up-and-coming band. Much is often made of new bands. As we all know, some make it, some just fade away. They all have to start somewhere. Over the summer I got my hands on the debut album by The Vaccines. I liked it straight away. It had a raw sound with a strong lively vocal and great guitars. Arguably they reminded me of the Ramones, whom I only saw the once, when they supported REM at Milton Keynes.

What I loved about The Vaccines was their edgy, youthful energy. I had seen it in many bands before. I was feeling energetic so I headed down the front. The band ran on stage and immediately picked up the vibe from an expectant crowd. As the musicians charged through their set, the crowd jumped, as one, for queen and country. I looked around at the youthful, sweaty faces with their bleary eyes. Each one was wrapped in their own trance, but we were as one, a hive of musos, simply having a good time. The gig reminded me of my early gigging days.

The Sunday show was very different. It was the return of the infamous madman of punk: Adam Ant. I never saw him first time round, partly because his health issues meant he wasn't allowed out very often; I can't ever recall him touring either. Some bands just float past. The good news is that he has managed to hold it together enough to go on tour. In fact he had come to the Junction in the spring, which I had missed due to a work commitment.

Now, the wonder of a weekend of live music was that both gigs were completely different in every way. The Vaccines were full of life, a roar of loud noise. Adam, though, while appearing healthy, probably had something like three decades of experience between him and his predecessors. While you would have thought youth would outplay age… it's not like that in rock music. The problem with a new band is that they simply don't have enough material to fill a set, unless they revert to covers. The Vaccines debut album *What Did You Expect from the Vaccines?* lasts less than thirty seven minutes and consists of 11 tracks. Their live show was timed at roughly sixty four minutes. While Adam Ant managed a quality two-hour set.

I came away with a simple message. Any gig can excite you, give you something to talk about, make you smile. A good gig, though, touches a nerve. It somehow reaches into your heart and gives you a little jolt. It might make you think, dream, sort out a problem or want to do something.

The brilliant gig does even more than this. It reaches deep into your soul. It gets right under your skin, sits back in a comfy chair and smiles. For ninety-odd minutes you reach outside yourself into the actual psyche of the band themselves. You see how and why they wrote that piece. You disappear from your world into theirs. It comes together and suddenly it all makes sense. At the end, like a wonderful train journey, you're brought safely home, back to where you stand. The trip makes you richer in mood, senses and emotions. For some, this journey might be painful, you might see things you'd rather not. On the other hand it might answer that nagging question or doubt in your mind. It might be the drawing back of a large velvet curtain, revealing that hidden door or shaft of sunlight.

For me, exceptional gigs have been rare. The exceptional gig depends so much on so many things. Much depends on how I am at that point in time. But they're made by the venue, the vibe of the people around me, the completeness of the show and, of course, a brilliant set of songs perfectly performed – and with a spectacular but appropriate light show. Many I've reported on in this book have been excellent, but even now I'm not sure whether I've yet seen the perfect gig.

At the end some bands simply let their anthem song roll, or throw their instruments on the ground, or simply wave goodnight. I end my show the only credible way I've seen. It's the final gesture at the end of an Ezio show. Ezio – Ezio Lunedei and Mark 'Booga' Fowell – are one of my favourite bands to see live. Both play truly superb guitar….Spanish flamenco/folky roots. They have strong local roots in Cambridge and Whittlesey and have built a solid, loyal following. In 1996 they survived the pressure of having one of their songs, "Cancel Today," selected by Tony Blair for his *Desert Island Discs*. World-wide fame never came; while I expect Ezio and Booga would be remarkable international stars, I sense they remain comfortable at simply being brilliant musicians who can open our hearts with their stories of real life *today*.

Ezio's shows are the most inclusive I've ever been to. The very best lead singers engage their crowd. Guy Garvey, Jim Kerr, Dave Gahan and Tim Booth beautifully draw their adoring fans to them. They spend quality time looking deep into the audience, even climbing in with them to make that vital connection.

Ezio is also wonderful at engagement. He tells us stories and exchanges banter with crowd. We end up calling out requests, which are played or ignored depending on his mood. There's no track list. Importantly while each track becomes a sing-along, you can see the emotion in everyone around you. We all get it.

Ezio has plenty of anthem songs – we usually end the night hollering out "Saxon Street" or "A Thousand Years." But they say farewell in a wonderfully mocking way. They come together, lock arms and bow. They then turn around with backs to us, the paying punters, and bow again. Brilliant.

If there was one gig to end this part of my journey then The Prodigy is as good as any to end on. You see, there are some bands who are simply awesome live. They have an energy, sound and power that others envy and try – but fail – to copy.

The amazing thing about The Prodigy is that they bring together everything I look for in a gig. They take no prisoners. They destroy your ears and deliver such a sound that you can't stand still.

Nic organised the tickets for this December gig show at what is one of my favourite London venues: the Brixton Academy. It turned out to be one of those late-night gigs. I thought 'late-nighters' were for weekends, but somehow The Prodigy managed to get three of them in a row… mid-week. When making the arrangements Nic casually announced they wouldn't be on till midnight.

'Bloody hell!' I thought. 'I'm shattered. I won't survive. It'll do me in.' Maybe I'm too old? A few days later I pulled myself together and said, 'fuck it. I can't miss that. The Prodigy, live and *in Brixton*. What happens if it's the perfect gig… the one I've been searching for?' – a search that has taken two-thirds of my life, vast sums of cash, lots of beer and, until recently, the inhaling of loads of smoke.

But real gig-goers have steel. They know the bigger prize. They know that The Gig is more important. I rallied myself and ventured south. Sophie, Nic, Julian and I met up in the Beehive pub, which is always entertaining. Tonight I found myself – being careful not to invade the top table, which was seated with locals and major dons – talking about anything and everything with a Jamaican philosopher.

Entry into the Academy has always been an experience. Everyone is body searched. But tonight the security search was heavier than any airport or border crossing. Even my wallet was pulled apart, which was a ploy, I bantered with the smiling muscle head, to nick my twenty quid. He didn't laugh.

Inside was an eager but good-tempered crowd. The place was already bouncing to the support act South Central. The strobes were in full effect, lighting up the Romeo and Juliet pale white balcony. We took our position to the right side of the stage, good for the girls' loo but not for the blokes'. But I like it on this side of this musical heaven.

I take my time to people-watch. There's a larger-than-expected number of girls here. Lots of small groups of mates laughing, hugging and, as their lager levels increase, pushing. The final support act, Caspa, prompts conversations with strangers, with whom I quickly discover a shared dislike for them. In front of me is a small group of youngish lads. Conversations are mixed and interesting. We discuss how many times we have seen The Prodigy. For the girl behind it's her first time. She shows me her Doc Martens. Why? I've no idea. She had black laces, not bright yellow. A novice.

Just after midnight the lights drop and a tremendous roar peels the fading paint from the balcony above. They're on. Within seconds we're all jumping around to "Voodoo People." The lads are being boisterous but nothing more than that. We crash into each other but it's controlled.

A small guy pushes past and whispers (if you can whisper against the sound screeching out of the amps)… he's selling pills. He's the pill seller.

'How on earth did he get in?' I thought to myself. It rather confirmed my suspicion that gangs run venues, hence the high level of door security… for most but not all.

The gig just flies past. The band pumps out hit after hit. The bass smashes into us. Before I know it we've had an hour of the show. For 60 minutes I hadn't stopped jumping up and down. As the lights behind the set beamed out, every hand was held high, reaching out.

Just before the encore, I felt a tap on my shoulder. Suddenly Nic, who had been a few feet behind me, was standing there. He was grinning so much his face looked ripped. His expression said it all. It was pure delight. He was totally into the event. Transfixed. He'd obviously gone through that moment when the gig takes you over. It takes control. You're in their hands. You want to scream forever. We hugged hard as the band closed on the trippy "Out of Space." The whole crowd, hands stretched skywards, were screaming the lyrics as if the world were going to end. A perfect way to finish. But most importantly, here I was at a gig, witnessing a fellow human being expressing all the emotions I thought were mine alone.

Suddenly I felt comforted. I was reassured that this passion for music, while personal, is something so many others pine for, dream of, live. I wasn't alone. I'm not totally demented. Others get it as well. This was it. This was a perfect gig.

Music means so much to me. I get the passion, I hear the screams, I dream I'm the character in the band's hit single. I know it gives me strength, a boost when I'm low, an injection of why life is worth living. Over the years I've cried, fallen over, got drenched in sweat and beer, got pissed but never passed out. Seeing bands play live has given me a reason for living. It has offered sanity in a complex, weird and frightening world. It has entered my soul and won't ever come out. I know I'm not alone. I know the passion for live music is alive and very well.

Someone once said to me: 'Aren't you getting too old for all this gig stuff?' I looked back, and without hesitating, said politely: 'No. I'll never stop.'

I need to see it live.

As we walked out into the night, the crowd had pretty much dispersed. A few headed off to the kebab van for a bag of chips. There was the echo of someone singing that final song. It had been a perfect gig tonight. The freezing winter evening made me put on the jumper I had tied round my waist earlier.

I boarded the night bus and headed over the Thames to the north side. My ears were tingling with the sound of the band,

and my head was churning over my back catalogue of past gigs. Suddenly a thought entered my head.

'So, what's next?'

Thank you

I would like to say a very special thank you to...

Jane Bromham for her wonderful cover designs, David Williams for providing editorial guidance and confidence in completing the book. Harriet Barcombe for proof reading my first draft. Keith Edwards for becoming our Glastonbury co-ordinator, Leslie and Paul Clarke for creating camp Glasto. Ken Ashford and Stuart Dunbar for laughing and making so many gigs and festivals memorable. Everyone involved with the Junction (Cambridge) in creating a local venue which has hosted so many bands (long may that continue), my wife Jenny for being so forgiving and Nick 'Nic' Crivich for being my muso and soul mate. Jim Fox for our midnight Manchester jams and Vj Krishnarayan for being Vj. And of course I'd like to thank every band I have ever seen as well as the promoters of gigs and festivals across the land.

Every effort has been made to record the correct date, time, place and band mentioned in this book. Everyone included in the narrative is a real person to the best of my memory. If I have made a mistake, I apologise. If you do note any errors, please do let me know. Enjoy the music.

Adam Broadway – March 2015